Indian Tales from Picuris Pueblo

For my friend
Dara Pelikan
with love –

Mary Wheeler

Dec. 25, 1990

ndian Tales *from* Picuris Pueblo

collected by
JOHN P. HARRINGTON
with musical transcriptions by
HELEN H. ROBERTS

edited by
MARTA WEIGLE

Ancient City Press
Santa Fe

International Standard Book Number:
Clothbound 0-941270-51-3
Paperback 0-941270-50-5
Library of Congress Catalogue Number:
88-072051

First Edition

Designed by Mary Powell

Cover photograph: An Isleta Boy. Photo by Edward S. Curtis from Volume 16 of *The North American Indian*, Norwood, Massachusetts, 1925. Courtesy of Mary Powell.

Frontispiece: Ramita and Juan José Martinez, potters. Picuris Pueblo, 1959. Photo by Mrs. John Champ. Courtesy Museum of New Mexico, Neg. No. 31041.

Contents

FOLKWAYS, collected by John P. Harrington
 from Rosendo Vargas

Preface

Picuris Pueblo is a remote northern New Mexico Indian community on the western slopes of the Sangre de Cristo Mountains in southern Taos County. Settled during the last half of the twelfth century, its population of some three thousand during the 1600s had declined dramatically by the early 1900s, when only one or two hundred people lived in the pueblo. Picuris residents speak a Northern Tiwa dialect that is closely related to the mutually intelligible Northern Tiwa spoken at Taos Pueblo, some twenty miles by trail to the north.

Before the 1920s or 1930s, most Picuris residents also spoke Spanish, since their church had until the late 1800s long served as a Spanish mission, San Lorenzo de Picurís, for both the pueblo and its more numerous Hispanic neighbors. The name Picuris is the Spanish *Picurís* (as used by Harrington), first recorded in the plural *Picuríes* by colonizer Don Juan de Oñate in 1598 and probably borrowed from the Jemez Pueblo term *pe·kwiles*, 'Picuris Indians'. The Picuris call themselves and their pueblo names that may be translated literally as 'mountain *wel*-people' and 'mountain *wel*-place' and which most likely refer to their home at the west end of a mountain pass leading to the Great Plains.

John Peabody Harrington, an ethnologist working for the Smithsonian Institution's Bureau of American Ethnology, collected, most likely in 1918, some four hundred pages of texts from Mr. Rosendo Vargas of Picuris Pueblo as part of his fieldwork on the language of Taos Pueblo. A remarkably gifted and prolific linguist, he recorded Vargas's stories, songs, and "folkways" accounts of Picuris life and later prepared them for bilingual publication in the *Forty-third Annual Report of the Bureau of American Ethnology* to the Secretary of the Smithsonian Institution, 1925-1926, published in 1928. Anthropologist and musicologist Helen H. Roberts provided musical transcriptions for the eleven songs in this collection, which appeared as part of "Picurís Children's Stories, with Texts and Songs." Her musicological "Analysis of Picurís Songs" concludes the essay.

Indian Tales from Picuris Pueblo reprints the English-language versions of the twenty-one "Children's Stories" and seven "Folkways" texts collected by Harrington. The eleven songs transcribed by Roberts have been reproduced from the 1928 publication. Harrington's introduction has been reprinted verbatim except that the footnotes have been incorporated into the Afterword and the chart, "Fig. 9.-The Picurís phonemes," has been eliminated. Other photographs of Picuris have been substituted throughout for the original Plate 43, "a view of the pueblo." Plate 44, a drawing depicting "The Contest Between Sengerepove'ena and the Giant" after the latter steals the former's wife, has been omitted. Because the Picuris language texts have not been reprinted here, an eighth and final "Folkways" text, the Picuris-language version of "The 'Our Father,' " does not appear. Because of the difficulty of reproducing Harrington's linguistic spelling of Picuris names and terms, only the most common diacritical markings are given in the texts and notes.

Harrington footnotes both the Picuris and the English versions of his stories and texts, and they are combined here. Those that are simple glosses, primarily the proper names, are bracketed in the texts that

Picuris Pueblo, 1941. Photo by T. Harmon Parkhurst. Courtesy Museum of New Mexico, Neg. No. 3346.

follow. Harrington uses the Spanish *estufa* instead of the more familiar "kiva" for the Pueblo Indians' ceremonial chamber, and this has been glossed only at its first appearance in a story. Harrington's more extensive footnotes appear in a separate section entitled "Notes on the Stories." For convenient reference, the editor has also listed pages numbers of the 1928 texts, characters in order of appearance, and the songs in each tale. The afterword provides further background on Harrington, Roberts, and their Picuris collection.

Santa Fe   Marta Weigle
December 1988

Aerial view of Picuris Pueblo, 1948. Photo made for Stanley Stubbs by Cutter-Carr Flying Service. Courtesy Museum of New Mexico, Neg. No. 3345.

Introduction

John P. Harrington

Among the Indians of the little Tiwa village of Picurís, which lies hidden among the mountains of northern New Mexico, the Earth is believed to sleep for about a month at the time of the winter solstice; that is the period for telling ancient myths. Some of the prettiest of these myths constitute the bulk of the present volume of texts. They are dictated by Rosendo Vargas just as he heard them told by his grandfather and others within the adobe walls of the home village when a boy "while the Earth was sleeping." They have all the savor of the New Mexican mountains and well illustrate the versatility of the language, which is capable of expressing the most intricate and poetic thought.

Characters which figure largely in the myths are the members of the family of cannibalistic Giants, the Elf (a youthful dwarf who has the strength of a man and goes about clad only in a breechclout), Fish Maiden, Sengerepove'ena (the Tewa hunter-adventurer), Shell Hat, the Sun, the Moon, the Morning Star, the Corn Maidens of the cardinal colors, the Butterflies of the cardinal colors, Magpietail Boy, Old Beaver, Old Wolf,

5

Old Coyote, Old Coyote Woman, the brother and sister Fawns, the Dove Maidens, Big Nostril, the Snakes, and several others. Most of the stories end with a good moral teaching or some explanation of nature, and then "You have a tail" — which means that it is your turn to tell a story. The songs which accompany the myths, charmingly rendered by Mr. Vargas, constitute one of the most pleasing features of the collection and have been transcribed by Miss Helen H. Roberts.

The dialect of Picurís and the markedly divergent Taos dialect make up the Northern Tiwa as contrasted with the Southern Tiwa or Isleteño. For further information on the classification of the Tanoan languages see my "Introductory Paper on the Tiwa Language, Dialect of Taos, New Mexico," in American Anthropologist, n. s., vol. 12, pp. 11–48, 1910.

At the end of the volume a number of nonmythological textlets dealing with folkways and an Our Father version, all from the same informant, have been added. The texts were originally prepared with interlinear translation, but this has been omitted because of the cost of printing, although I believe that the including of interlinear translation best subserves the purpose for which such texts are published.

Grateful acknowledgment is due especially to Dr. J. Walter Fewkes, Chief of the Bureau of American Ethnology, for his sympathetic support of these studies. The warmest thanks are also given to Rosendo Vargas, the narrator, and Miss Helen H. Roberts, who transcribed the songs with painstaking accuracy.

Children's Stories

Collected by John P. Harrington
from Rosendo Vargas

MAGPIETAIL BOY AND HIS WIFE

Once upon a time[1] the people were dwelling at Picurís Pueblo. And Magpietail Boy and his wife, Yellow Corn Woman,[2] dwelt there. Yellow Corn Woman belonged to the Society of Wizards.[3] Down below at Yawatceke'ai[4] they had their estufa [kiva].[5] Yellow Corn Woman went there every night where the Wizards were doing their sacred ceremonies. Magpietail Boy liked to sleep so much that he did not know where his wife went in the evenings nor at what time of the night she returned. As soon as it got dark, Yellow Corn Woman went over to where the Wizards had their estufa, to take part in their sacred ceremonies. At times she would come home after midnight, and at other times she would come home when it was already daylight, in the early morning. But her husband, Magpietail Boy, was such a sleepyhead that he did not know what time his wife came home; neither did he know where she was going every night.

But one time he said to himself, "Suppose I do not sleep to-night, in order to see where it is that my wife is going out to nightly. To-night I will follow her. When I lie down in bed this evening I will pretend that I am asleep. As soon as she goes out of the house I will follow right behind her wherever she goes."

And that evening, after his wife had given him his supper, she said to him: "My husband, you must be lying down, for the time has come for you to sleep." Magpietail Boy made believe that he was very sleepy and said: "All right, my wife. I am really very sleepy, so now I am going to lie down." And so saying, he lay down. He was lying in bed pretending that he was asleep. He was snoring away.

His wife, Yellow Corn Woman, began to hurry to get ready to leave. Shortly somebody knocked at the door. Yellow Corn Woman opened the door. And Magpietail Boy heard someone telling his wife, "Hurry. You are the only one who is late." Magpietail Boy recognized the person's voice that was speaking outside. He said to himself, "I believe my wife is doing ceremonies with the Wizards, but I will follow her to-night. To-night I shall know." Yellow Corn Woman, dressed up well, her hair well combed, went out of the house. As soon as she had gone out, Magpietail Boy got out of bed, dressed up, and followed his wife.

Yellow Corn Woman went southwest, walking fast as she went along the trail. As the moon was shining, her moccasins looked white as snow, as she came to the estufa of the Wizards. Magpietail Boy watched his wife as she entered a place which was brightly lighted. "I see that this is the place where this wife of mine has been coming every night, doing ceremonies with the Wizards. But I will hide myself under here." As he said thus he hid himself near the roof-hole.[6] He put himself under the roof-hole sticks.[7]

When he looked into the estufa the Wizards had it lighted up. Shortly they began to prepare themselves for the ceremony. Some took their eyes out, some took their noses off, some took their ears off, some took their legs off, and some even cut themselves in two. They were all fixing themselves in various ways. After they were finished dressing, they were told by their leader, "Now let us start our ceremony." As he said thus they put a rainbow across the estufa. Then they began to do their ceremony. As they tried to climb the rainbow, they would fall back again. Their leader said to them, "I believe there is a person near who is not our equal. Suppose that one of you go out to see." And one of them went out to look. He looked around among the bushes, but he could not see anything, so he went back into the estufa again. "There is not a human being outside," he told the leader.

Then they again started to do their ceremony. They began to climb the rainbow. Again they fell back. They could not climb the rainbow. "Stop for a moment," said the leader. "There must be some human being near who is not our equal. That is the reason that we have failed in doing our ceremony. Suppose we call the Screech Owl, for he is the only one who can see, even in the dark." Then they called the Screech Owl. "Screech Owl, we have called you because you are the chief of the night, since you are the only one that can see in the dark. You can even see a little ant very far in the dark. You are the chief of the night. There is a human being near who is not our equal, and that is the reason we have failed to do our ceremony. So that is why we have called you here." "Hu, hu," said the Screech Owl as he flew outside. He lighted around in the weeds and bushes there, but he could not see a human being. And as he was going into the estufa to report that he had not seen anything, he noticed there at the roof-hole the tail of a wolf hide sticking out through the roof-hole sticks. He then went into the estufa and said to the Wizards: "Hu, hu. I have not seen a human being outside, but there is the tail of a wolf skin sticking out from under the roof-hole sticks," And saying "Hu, hu," he flew out.

As soon as the Screech Owl mentioned the wolf skin Yellow Corn Woman realized who it was. "That must be my husband then," she said to herself. "Let one of you go out to see. If you should find anybody, bring him in," said the leader. And one of them went out to look. As he looked around the roof-hole, there was indeed a person under the roof-hole, covered with a wolf skin and hidden under the roof-hole sticks. He was taken out of there, was carried into the estufa, and was brought to where the leader was sitting. "Ah, how is it that you come about my precinct?" But Magpietail Boy did not say anything. He was then taken over and seated where his wife was seated. As it was then after midnight, he could hardly keep his eyes open. He finally laid his head on his wife's lap and went to sleep. After the Wizards had finished their ceremony, they made a ridge-bench in the arroyo. He was then put there while he was still asleep.

When he awoke early the next morning he was lying face up in a strange place on the cliff bench. "How am I going to get out of this place, now?" he said to himself. It was even impossible for him to turn over. Since the cliff bench on which he was lying was only wide enough for him to lie on, he could only look upward as he lay there.

Now at Pethentha ["Deer Home"] there dwelt an Elf. "I believe I will go for a walk down southwest to the river to–day." As he said thus, he started out. Going along he sang:

NO. 1. TRAVELING SONG OF THE ELF[8]

Transcription by Helen H. Roberts.

11

As he sang, he passed right above where Magpietail Boy was lying, and Magpietail Boy cried from below: "Whoever you are that is singing along, stop, and get me out of this place." The Elf heard the cry and went to see the place where it sounded. As he peeped into the cliff, he saw Magpietail Boy lying on the cliff bench. "Ah, Magpietail Boy, what are you doing here?" Magpietail Boy said to him: "Elf, get me out of this place." "You will have to wait, for I am going down southwest to the river, since I am paying courtship to a maiden, but I will return shortly." As he said thus, the Elf went down southwest to the river. He went along singing:

NO. 2. LOVE SONG OF THE ELF[9]

rai - ya - 'e-hyo 'ai - hyo wi-ro - he - e - yo   Ya - 'e-he - 'a 'e-rai-

hyo - 'e - ro   ya - 'e - he - 'a 'e-rai - hyo - 'e - ro   Ya-

'e - he - 'a 'e - ra - i - hyo - 'e - ro   ya - 'e - he - 'a 'e - ra - i -

hyo - 'e - ro   'E - rai - ya - 'e-hyo 'ai - hyo wi - ro -

he - e - yo   Ha - a - te - e pa - am - 'o - nę ha-

a - te - e pa - am - 'o - nę   Ką - ą - mą - ąn tce - el -

tci - i - są tə - ə - pi - u 'ąn - - mę - ę - tci 'E -

rai - ya - 'e - hyo 'ai - hyo wi - ro - he - e - yo   Ya - 'e - he - 'a 'e - rai

hyo - 'e - ro   ya - 'e - he - 'a 'e - rai - hyo - 'e - ro   Ya-

'e - he - 'a 'e - ra - i - hyo - 'e - ro   ya - 'e - he - 'a 'e - ra - i -

hyo - 'e - ro   'E - rai - ya - 'e - hyo 'ai - hyo wi - ro - he - e - yo.

13

As he went along, he came to where Fish Maiden was basking beside the river. "Good morning, Fish Maiden," he said. "Come over this way," said the Fish Maiden to him. The Elf went over and they both sat down to talk. As the Fish Maiden was getting dry, her mouth began to open. "I must be going back into the water where I belong." The Elf said: "Could you not stand it a little while longer?" The Fish Maiden said: "I do not stay outside of the water so very long. That is the reason that I am already about to go back in." Because the Fish Maiden did not want to stay outside the water, the Elf went away angry.

As he went he came to a tall spruce tree and there he picked five spruce cones, and went over to where Magpietail Boy was. As he came to the place, he said to Magpietail Boy: "I now perhaps might help you to get out of there, if you can catch one of the five spruce cones. So I am going to drop them to you, one at a time. If you miss all of them, you will not get out of there." "Very well, indeed, I will try my best to catch them." And so the Elf dropped one of the spruce cones, but he did not catch it. He dropped him another, but he did not catch this one either. He dropped him the third one, but he did not catch it either. Now the Elf began to scare him by saying: "You must do your best, for this one is the last." "Yes, I will," said Magpietail Boy. He then dropped him the fourth one. He did not catch it. "Then you can stay there; that is all I had," the Elf said to him. Magpietail Boy said nothing, but looked very frightened as he was lying there. The Elf then took out another spruce cone. "Now, this time I am not telling you a lie. That is the last. If you do not catch this one, I can not get you out of there." As the Elf said thus, he dropped the last one that he had. But

Magpietail Boy caught this one somehow. "All right," said the Elf. "You must drop this right straight down from where you are lying." Then he dropped it, as he was told, and shortly there came up a spruce tree loaded with branches, right beside him, until it reached up to the bench. "Now," said the Elf, "you must climb this spruce tree and get out." Then Magpietail Boy came out. "Thank you for helping me," he said to the Elf. He then told the Elf just what had happened to him that night and how he had gotten in there. "Very well," said the Elf. Then they went over to where there was a fallen tree. The Elf found a woodworm and gave it to Magpietail Boy, telling him: "You must put this worm by your wife's bed to-night. This will fix her. So you must go home, but you must not tell your wife. You must not try to quarrel with her. This worm will do enough to her." As the Elf told him that, he went to his home.

When Magpietail Boy arrived home, he sat down very quiet. His wife brought him something to eat, and after he had eaten, since it was already night, they both went to bed. And he laid the worm above where his wife slept. The worm entered Yellow Corn Woman at her navel. While she was sleeping it ate up all her entrails and she died. And after that Magpietail Boy lived happily, alone.

You have a tail.[10]

SENGEREPOVE'ENA FIGHTS WITH THE SUN

Once upon a time the people were dwelling at San Juan Pueblo. And Sengerepove'ena[11] dwelt there with his wife and two children. Sengerepove'ena was a great hunter. That was the only way he fed his children. Every day he went out hunting and brought deer.

Once he went out hunting and could not find any deer. All day he walked. Not a track of deer could he see. And as he was tired he sat down to rest on a log. "But why do I not find any deer to-day?" he said. He took his bow. He drew his bow, saying: "Would that a four-horned deer might come out. I could shoot him at once and knock him down." Then exactly as he said, a four-horned deer came out. He aimed. But while he was drawing his bow, the Deer spoke to him. "My friend, do not shoot me." Sengerepove'ena, still drawing his bow, sat frightened. The Deer went to where he was sitting. "My friend," said the Deer to him, "let me talk to you. Within five days from to-day you must make arrows. You must also make five quivers. When you finish these quivers you must be ready. This Sun that is helping us to live and giving us light is about to make war on you. That is why within five days you must come this way again, with your children. Here you will meet with the Sun. Here you will have a fight. That is all that I have to tell you. You must act like a man." Then Sengerepove'ena got up from where he was sitting and started home.

He was not bringing any deer. "Much as he has been hunting, he never has come home from hunting without a deer," the people said when they saw him coming from hunting. "Sengerepove'ena is not bringing a deer this time," the people said as they saw him.

When he reached home he put his quiver away. He sat down very sad. "My husband," said his wife, "why did you not kill a deer to-day? There must be something the matter with you. As long as you have been going out hunting, you never have come back without a deer." She placed something to eat, and he sat down to eat. He put something into his mouth two or three times and got up. "My wife," said he to the woman, "while I was hunting, just as I was about to shoot a Deer, that Deer spoke to me and began to talk to me, telling me that five days from to-day the Sun that is giving us light is going to make war on me. He also told me that within five days from to-day I must make five quivers and fill them with arrows. And the Deer told me to go to the same place I saw him to-day five days from to-day and that there the Sun and I will meet, and there we will have a fight. So you also must get ready. You must also have the two children ready."

Then Sengerepove'ena did nothing but make arrows during the five days, and the night of the fourth day Sengerepove'ena had five quivers ready, filled with arrows. He said: "We shall see in the morning who is the braver; we shall see who is more of a man, the Sun or I."

Before daylight the next day they got up and ate breakfast. Then Sengerepove'ena put his war paint on. He painted his face with red, his body with white in blotches. "Come on, let us go, my dear ones, no matter what happens to me. My wife, if I should be injured in any way or killed, you must take these two children that we have to where their grandfather and grandmother live. There you may live. They will take care of you."

Then they started out and when they reached the place where the Deer had spoken a tall man came out in the northeast, he also being in war paint, with an eagle feather at the back of his head and with a shining ornament on his forehead. Then they began to shoot at each other from a distance. They came closer to each other in a short time. As they began to get closer, they were emptying their quivers. But they could not hit each other. They were getting nearer. Now each had only one quiver left. But they could not hit each other. They were still getting nearer. Now each had only two or three arrows left. They still got nearer. Each shot his last arrow. They began to have a hand-to-hand fight. There they wrestled. And then Sengerepove'ena was thrown down. When he was thrown down the Sun took out his knife and severed Sengerepove'ena's neck. As soon as his neck was severed the two children left their mother and ran away to their grandparents. Then the Sun took their mother up to the heaven where he lives. The Sun also took Sengerepove'ena's head with him.

The children reached their grandparents' home. There they lived. As they grew older they often asked their grandparents where their parents were. Their grandparents said to them: "My little children, you will never see your parents again." Then the children said: "But anyway we are going to look for our parents until we can find them." Their grandparents said to them: "My little children, you will never find your parents. The Sun whom you see above the clouds has taken them to his home." The children said: "But we are going to look for them until we find them." "Very well," said their grandfather, "go into the woods and cut plenty of willow trees. But you must not go to or cut the willows where the Sun killed your father."

Then the children took their knives and went to the woods to cut willows. One of them said: "Why does not our grandfather want us to cut the willows where our father was killed? We will go there anyway and get the willows there." They went there. When they came to the place where their father was killed, they found willows. And one of them began to cut them. The willow tree said to them: "My children, why are you cutting my flesh?" The children looked frightened, but they went home and told their grandfather. "Grand-father, the willows spoke to us and told us, 'Why are you cutting my flesh?'" Their grandfather said to them: "I have told you not to go there. Now you can go this other way to cut willows." Then the two children took their knives again and went to cut willows. When they came to the woods they began to cut willows. They took the willows in their arms and carried them to their grandfather.

"Very well," said their grandfather, "now I shall make shinny sticks for you. When I finish your shinny sticks you can take them and go to look for your parents. While you are looking for your parents you will need them." The grandfather finished the shinny sticks and they put them on their backs and went to look for their parents.

They were on the road about three or four days. They came to the home of Old Male Woodrat and Old Female Woodrat. The Woodrats said to them: "Little children, where are you going?" "We are going to look for our parents," said the boys to the Woodrats. "Very well," said the Woodrats. And each took two little sticks from his ears and gave one to each of the boys, saying to them, "You will need this where you are hunting for your parents. If there should be any betting, you could rub them on yourselves."

Then the little boys went. As they went they came to the home of the White Butterflies.[12] "Where are you going, little boys?" the White Butterflies said to them.

"We are going to look for our parents," said the little boys to the White Butterflies. "Very well," said the White Butterflies, "if you take this white paint, where you are going to look for your parents you may need it." They took the white paint and went.

As they went, they came to the home of the Black Butterflies. The Black Butterflies said to them: "Where are you going, little boys?" "We are going to look for our parents," said the little boys to the Black Butterflies. "Very well," said the Black Butterflies, "if you take this black paint, where you are going to look for your parents you may need it." The little boys took the black paint and went.

As they went, they came to the home of the Yellow Butterflies. The Yellow Butterflies said to them: "Where are you going, little boys?" "We are going to look for our parents," said the little boys to the Yellow Butterflies. "Very well," said the Yellow Butterflies, "if you take this yellow paint, where you are going to look for your parents you may need it." The little boys took the yellow paint and went.

As they went, they came to the home of the Blue Butterflies. The Blue Butterflies said to them: "Where are you going, little boys?" "We are going to look for our parents," said the little boys to the Blue Butterflies. "Very well," said the Blue Butterflies, "if you take this blue paint, where you are going to look for your parents you may need it." The little boys took the blue paint and went.

As they went, they came to where there was a certain Flying Creature which looked like a crow. "Where are you going, little boys?" the Flying Creature said to them. "We are going to look for our parents," said the little boys. "Very well," said the Flying Creature, "have you any white, black, and yellow paint?" The little boys said, "We have." "Good," said the Flying Creature, "if you can paint my feathers I will take you up to where the Sun lives." "Good. We will paint your feathers any way you wish." "Very well," said the Flying Creature, "you can paint my head white and my bill and legs yellow, and here on my breast white, and the tail white, and black at the end. After you paint me as I have told you, I will be ready to fly." "Very well," the little boys said, "we will paint you any way you wish." They took out their paint and painted the Flying Creature as he had told them. After they finished painting him, he was called by them the Eagle. That is the reason the Eagle looks that way. "Very well," said the Eagle, "sit on my back. Hold on tight, I am about to fly. As soon as I fly, close your eyes. You must not look until I tell you." "Very well," said the little boys.

They sat on the Eagle's back and the Eagle flew. He ascended higher and higher and kept circling. Then he lighted. "Now you can open your eyes," he said to the little boys.

When they opened their eyes they were in a strange-looking land. "Now, little boys, I have brought you to the Sun's land. Over there where that white house is your mother is staying. She is now the Sun's wife, and your father's head is at the Morning Star's house. Every morning the Morning Star plays shinny with your father's head. So you must go early to-morrow morning to the place where he is playing shinny. He makes a fierce noise, but you must not fear him. Should he ask you questions, you must not fear to answer him. If he should ask you to play shinny, you must be willing to play shinny with him. But you must not hit your father's head. You must only try to hit his shinny sticks.

He has only about ten shinny sticks. When you break his last shinny stick the Morning Star will drop dead. When he drops dead you must take your father's head and come here again. I will be waiting here."

The little children went as the Eagle had told them. Early in the morning they heard a fierce noise. "There is the Morning Star playing shinny with our father's head," said the little children; "indeed, let us go and meet him. We will do as the Eagle told us, and will win." They went where the Morning Star was making the noise. When they came to where the Morning Star was the Morning Star said to them: "Little boys, why do you come here? There is no creature that comes around where I am; not even a little bird comes around here. Now I shall eat you both up." "We are around here, anyhow," the little boys said. "Very well," said the Morning Star, "this is your father's head, and I play shinny with it every morning. If you are around here looking for your parents, let us play shinny with your father's head. Whoever wins shall have the head."

Then they began to play shinny. The little children, instead of hitting the shinny ball, were hitting the Morning Star's shinny sticks. When his last shinny stick was broken, the Morning Star dropped dead. "We win," said the little boys. "Our father's head we shall take over to where the Eagle is waiting for us." So they took the head and came to where the Eagle was waiting.

"How did you make out, little boys?" said the Eagle to them. "Well," said the little boys, "we have won our father's head." "Very well," said the eagle, "now you may go and get your mother. When you bring her back here I will take you down again to the earth. You must go to where your mother is staying after it gets dark, for that is the only time that the Sun goes to sleep. While he is asleep you must spit the earsticks that the Woodrats gave you on him and he will not wake up, and then you must bring your mother here." "All right," said the little boys, "as soon as it grows dark we shall go over to where our mother is living."

When it got dark, they went. When they entered the room they found the Sun asleep. They spit on him with the earsticks of the Woodrats. The Sun fell fast asleep. They took their mother out and carried her to where the Eagle was waiting for them.

"How did you make out, little boys?" said the Eagle. "Well," said the little boys. "Very well," said the Eagle, "the three of you sit on my back, close your eyes as soon as I fly, do not open your eyes until I land on the ground." Then they got on the back of the Eagle, and the Eagle flew. He circled around and landed on the ground. "Now," said the Eagle, "you can take your father's head home. When you reach home you must put your father's head in a dark place. Don't look at it for five days. By that time your father will turn to flesh again."

The litle children and their mother went home. When they reached home they put their father's head in a dark place, as the Eagle had told them. After five days they looked where they had put the head and they found Sengerepove'ena as he had looked before. They lived happily ever afterward.

You have a tail.

The Old Giant Steals Sengerepove'ena's Wife

Once upon a time at San Juan the people dwelt. And also Sengerepove'ena and White Corn Woman, his wife, dwelt there. Sengerepove'ena was a hunter. He did nothing but hunt. He went hunting every day and brought deer.[13] And his wife did nothing but wash clothes down at the river.

And once Sengerepove'ena went out hunting. White Corn Woman went to the river to wash clothes. While she was washing her clothes the Old Giant came to her. "What are you doing?" said the Giant to her. "I am washing clothes," said White Corn Woman. "Very well, get into this packbasket then," said the Giant. "I am already starting home. My husband comes home from hunting at this time," said White Corn Woman. "Get into this packbasket, I said. If you do not get in I will take you and put you in myself," said the Giant. "I am already starting home. My husband comes home from hunting at this time," said White Corn Woman. Then the Giant took her and put her into the packbasket and started for his home.

When Sengerepove'ena returned from hunting his wife was not at home. "But why is it that my wife does not come up from the river early this time? I think I will go down to the river and see." As he said thus, he went down to the river to look. When he came to her place of washing, the pot was still there and her clothes were still hanging to dry as she had left them. "But where did my wife go?" said Sengerepove'ena.

As he was walking around there he found a track of the Giant. "I think this big person has stolen my wife. But anyhow I will follow him until I catch up with him." He put his quiver on his back and started to follow the tracks of the Giant.

As he went he came to the home of old Male Woodrat and Old Female Woodrat. "Sengerepove'ena, where are you going?" the Woodrat said to him. "I am going to fetch my wife, because the Old Giant has stolen my wife from me." "Yes, he was passing here to-day. 'The one greedy for people is taking a person,' the people called out to him as he was going by here." Old Male Woodrat and Old Female Woodrat each gave him an earstick. "In case of betting you must spit on yourself with this," Old Male Woodrat said. And Old Male Woodrat took out a tobacco bag and also gave him a pipe and told him: "You may take this pipe in case of betting."

As he went he came to the home of the White Butterflies. "Sengerepove'ena, where are you going?" said the White Butterflies to him. Sengerepove'ena said: "The Old Giant has stolen my wife and I am going to fetch her." "You can bring her back. 'The one greedy for people is taking a person,' the people called out to him as he passed here." The White Butterflies fed him white cornbread and white boiled beans. After he had eaten he then set off again to follow the tracks of the Giant.

Then Sengerepove'ena went on. As he went he came to the home of the Black Butterflies. "Sengerepove'ena, where are you going?" said the Black Butterflies to him. Sengerepove'ena said: "The Old Giant has stolen my wife. I am going to fetch her back." The Black Butterflies said: "'The one greedy for people is taking a person,' the people said to him as he passed." The Black Butterflies fed him black cornbread and black boiled beans. After he had eaten he then set off again to follow the tracks of the Giant.

As he went he came to the home of the Yellow Butterflies. "Sengerepove'ena, where are you going?" said the Yellow Butterflies to him. Sengerepove'ena said: "The Old Giant has stolen my wife and I am going to fetch her." "You can bring her. 'The one greedy for people is taking a person,' the people said to him as he passed," said the Yellow Butterflies. He was fed yellow cornbread and yellow boiled beans. After he had eaten he again started off to follow the tracks of the Giant.

As he went, he came to the home of the Blue Butterflies. "Sengerepove'ena, where are you going?" said the Blue Butterflies to him. "The Old Giant has stolen my wife. I am going to fetch my wife." "You can bring her. 'The one greedy for people is taking a person,' the people here said to him as he went," said the Blue Butterflies. He was fed blue cornbread and blue boiled beans. After he had eaten he again followed the tracks of the Giant.

At last he came to the home of the Giant. As he entered the house he found his own wife in the house. "My wife, what are you doing here?" he said to his wife. "While I was washing at the river the Giant came and put me into his packbasket and brought me here. The Giant is there in his estufa [kiva]," said his wife to him. "Very well," said Sengerepove'ena, "I will go down to the estufa and you can be getting ready. After I kill him, we can go home."

And then Sengerepove'ena went down into the estufa, in where the Giant was. Entering there he found the Giant lying leaning asleep. "Sengerepove'ena, why are you entering here in my private place? There is no living creature that comes around here. Not even a little bird comes here," the Giant said to him. "Because you have stolen my wife, that is the reason I have come to get her," Sengerepove'ena said to the Giant. "Very well," said the Giant, "we will bet. The one that wins shall have the woman." "Very well," said Sengerepove'ena.

Ladder and kiva opening, Picuris Pueblo, April 1970. Photo by LeRoy D. Moloney. Courtesy Museum of New Mexico, Neg. No. 53186.

The Giant took out a long pipe and said: "The one that fills this estufa to the top with a cloud of smoke from the pipe shall win." As he said this, he lighted his pipe. Then he began to make the cloud of smoke from his pipe. But before the smoke reached halfway up the estufa his tobacco burned out from his pipe.

Now Sengerepove'ena's turn came. He began to spit on his pipe with the earsticks that the Old Woodrats had given him, and began to put tobacco into it. His pipe was not larger than his little finger. "Wu, you could not do half as well as I did. The smoke of your pipe will never reach the ceiling, because your pipe is too small. Even my pipe, large as it is, did not get half way. Now I am going to win the woman from you." Sengerepove'ena then lighted his pipe and began to make a cloud of smoke. Slowly it rose halfway. In a short time it reached up to the roof-hole. "I think you must have more power than I," said the Giant to him. "But you have not defeated me yet. Now we shall see. Whoever comes out safe shall have the woman."

Then the Giant took a bag of obsidians from a shelf hole in the wall and said: "Now this will cut you to pieces. And so it will be your turn this time. The one that comes out alive from this estufa shall have the woman. You are to stay in here first." "Very well," said Sengerepove'ena. He spit on himself with the earsticks which the Old Woodrats had given him. The Old Giant started to burn the obsidians and went outside. The obsidians began to explode in the estufa like a gun. "Now those will cut Sengerepove'ena to pieces. Now I shall have the woman." After the obsidians were all exploded, the Giant went into the estufa. But when he went in Sengerepove'ena was still sitting there as if nothing had happened. "Now it is your turn," Sengerepove'ena said to the Giant. He then took out the obsidians and set them afire, and then went outside. The obsidians were exploding like a gun in the estufa.

"Now let us go," he said to his wife, "the Giant has now been cut all to pieces by the obsidians." With his wife he then set out.

As they went they came to the home of the Blue Butterflies. "Sengerepove'ena, are you already taking your wife?" said the Blue Butterflies to him. "Yes," said Sengerepove'ena. "You must hurry then. His flesh was all cut to pieces but will all come together again in a short time."

And then they went and came to the home of the Yellow Butterflies. "Sengerepove'ena, are you already taking your wife?" "Yes," said Sengerepove'ena. "You must hurry then. His flesh was all cut to pieces but is coming together again already," the Yellow Butterflies told them, and they went.

They came there to the home of the Black Butterflies. "Sengerepove'ena, are you already taking your wife?" said the Black Butterflies to him. "Yes," said Sengerepove'ena. "You must hurry then. His flesh was all cut to pieces but has come together again already." And as they were told that they went.

They came there to the home of the White Butterflies. "Sengerepove'ena, are you already taking your wife?" said the White Butterflies to him. "Yes," said Sengerepove'ena. "You must hurry then. His flesh was all cut to pieces but has come together again already." And as they were told that they went.

They came there to the home of Old Male Woodrat and Old Female Woodrat. "Sengerepove'ena, are you already taking your wife?" the Woodrats said to him. "Yes," said Sengerepove'ena. "You must hurry then.

His flesh was all cut to pieces but it has come together and now he is coming tracking you." As they were told this they went.

The Old Giant put his packbasket on his back and started to track Sengerepove'ena. As it was hot, he was sweating as he went along the road.

He then called a Buzzard. The Buzzard soon came to him. "What is the matter, Phutetala[14]?" said the Buzzard to him. "I am calling you because Sengerepove'ena has stolen a pretty woman from me, to see if you can make it hot, so that I can catch them wherever they sit down to rest in the shade and take the woman away from him." "I do not like very much heat, as I am bald-headed." As the Buzzard said this he flew away.

In a little while the Buzzard called the heat. The Giant was sweating as he went along the road. "Sengerepove'ena and his wife must stand heat well," said he as he sat down to rest from the heat under a cotton-wood tree. Sengerepove'ena and his wife were going along feeling nice and cool.

After a while the Giant called a Crow. While he was sitting there under the shade of the cottonwood tree the Crow came to him. "What is the matter, Phutetala?" said the Crow to him. "I have called you so that you can summon the rain. Sengerepove'ena has stolen a pretty woman from me, and I am tracking them. I might be able to catch him wherever they stop for shelter from the rain, and take the woman away from him." "I do not like the rain, because if my wings get wet I soon tire of flying," said the Crow, and flew away.

In a little while the Crow called the rain. It began to get cloudy and the rain soon began to pour. It rained, together with thunder. The Giant was drenched as he went along the road. The lightning struck in front of his face, and as it struck he closed his eyes. And when he heard the noise of the thunder he jumped as he went along there drenched. Sengerepove'ena and his wife were going along the road feeling nice and cool. As the Old Giant went along the road drenched he said to himself, "Sengerepove'ena must stand rain well for I have not been able to overtake him yet. I think I will turn back again. Why am I going, drenched as I am, and with the roads muddy?" And the Giant returned again to his home.

Sengerepove'ena and his wife arrived home and they lived happily thereafter.

And this is why the Giant has never again come to San Juan to look for more people, since he suffered so much from the heat and rain.

You have a tail.

The Old Giantess and the Brother and Sister Fawns

Long ago the Old Giantess lived at Wetholapawa'an ["Pine Footleg"]. She went out hunting every day and killed whatever she could out there and brought it home, such as rabbits, chipmunks, tree squirrels, or whatever animals she could get while going about hunting.

Putting her shawl over her shoulders and taking her cane, she once started for Pin'oma. While she was walking about at Pin'oma, she found two little Fawns fast asleep. Going over slowly and quietly toward where they were lying asleep, she approached them, covered the young Fawns with the shawl which she had on her shoulders, and caught them. "Hurrah! I have got the little Fawns," the Old Giantess said to herself, "now I

shall take them home and fatten them up and eat them."
She wrapped them up in her shawl, put them on her
back, and carried them home.

After she brought the little Fawns home, she turned
them loose inside the house, and they walked about.
She fed them with corn mush and what else she could
every morning. That is how she nursed them. Little
by little the young Fawns began to grow. As they grew
older, they got accustomed to the house. The Old
Giantess used to take them outside for pleasure every
day, and they played around there. They would walk
up the road for a distance and then return again. As
the Old Giantess fed them, they slowly grew larger.
Every day the Old Giantess would say to them: "Little
ones, I believe your little kidneys are already pretty fat."
Thus she would say to them as she felt their little kidneys. And the little Fawns said to each other: "Let us
run away from the Old Giantess, for she tells us every
day that our little kidneys are already fat, and is likely
to roast us and eat us up." In a short time the little
Fawns began to get more afraid. One night they said
to each other: "To-morrow we must run away, lest the
Old Giantess roast us and devour us."

The next morning the Old Giantess gave them their
breakfast and took them outside to play as usual. "Now
let us run away. We will walk up the road where we
usually go, but this time we will go and will not return."
As they said thus, they started off. The Old Spider
Woman, who happened to live near by, was sitting for
pleasure on the roof of her house. As she watched the
little Fawns going along the road, she said: "The little
Fawns of the Old Giantess are running away." When
the Old Giantess heard this, she said to herself: "They
go as far as the top and then come back again." The

little Fawns were already going quite a distance up the road. Old Spider Woman was heard saying again from the top of her house: "The little Fawns of the Old Giantess are running away." Old Spider Woman kept repeating this every once in a while. "It must be so," said the Old Giantess, as she put her shawl on her shoulders, took her cane, went outside her house, and saw that her Fawns were already quite a distance away. "Sure enough, my Fawns are running away." As she said thus, she followed the Fawns.

The little Fawns went along and came to Paxepeta on the river. Going on, they came to where Big Nostril[15] had his blanket spread out and was looking for lice. "What is the matter, little ones? Where are you going?" Big Nostril said to them. "We are running away because the Old Giantess threatened to kill us, feeling our little kidneys every day. So please hide us." "Very well," said Big Nostril, "enter my nostrils." So the little Fawns went into his nostrils. In a short time the Old Giantess came, all sweating, to where Big Nostril was sitting hunting lice. "Big Nostril, I am following my Fawns, who are running away from me. Have you not seen them here?" said the Old Giantess. "No Fawns have come to me, as I am doing nothing but looking for lice." He sneezed. "For pity's sake, Big Nostril, my Fawns are going along over yonder." The little Fawns were going at quite a distance. The Old Giantess, sweating, followed behind them.

As the little Fawns went along, they came to where Old Plowmaker[16] was making a plow. "What is the matter, little ones? Where are you going?" the Old Plowmaker said as he looked at his plow on both sides to see if it was true. "We are running away because the Old Giantess threatened to kill us, feeling our little kidneys every day. So please hide us," said the little Fawns. "Very well, both of you enter this crack in the plow." So both of the little Fawns entered. In a short time the Old Giantess came along, all sweating, with her shawl on her shoulders, to where the Old Plowmaker was making a plow.[17] "Plowmaker, have you not seen my Fawns around here?" said the Old Giantess. "I am doing nothing but making plows, and have not seen any little Fawns," he said, as he looked to see if the plow was true. "Tiu tiu take, tiu tiu take,[18]" went the Old Plowmaker. "For pity's sake, Plowmaker, my Fawns are going along over yonder," said she. The little Fawns were going at quite a distance along the road. The Old Giantess, all sweating, again followed behind the Fawns.

The Fawns came to the dam where Beaver was lying basking beside the water. "What is the matter, little ones? Where are you going?" said the Old Beaver to them. "We are running away because the Old Giantess threatened to kill us, feeling our little kidneys every day. So please carry us across to the other side of the river," said the little Fawns to the Old Beaver. "Very well then," said the Old Beaver, "get on my back and I will take you across the river." So the little fawns got on his back and he carried them across the river, and Old Beaver told them: "You must go over to Kuhane'ai where the Snakes live. They will tell you where to go." As the Old Beaver told them thus, the Fawns went on. In a short time the Old Giantess came, all sweating, with her shawl on her shoulders, to where Old Beaver was basking beside the river. "Old Beaver, have you not seen my Fawns around here?" "Yes, I just carried them across the river. They are still going near." "Well then, carry me across also, so that I can catch them before they get too far away from me," said the Old

Giantess. "Get on my back then," said the Old Beaver. As she got on his back, he started to carry her across. But as the Beaver came to the middle of the river, where it was deeper, he turned himself upside down. "P'axalamummun, P'axalamummun,[19]" went the Old Giantess as she was sinking under the water and again emerging. But she finally reached the shore and came out of the water, all drenched, and she said: "For pity's sake! How annoying it is when one is trying to do something to make a living. My Fawns are gradually getting farther away from me." She shook herself and again began to follow the Fawns.

The Fawns went over to Kuhane'ai, where the Snakes lived, as the Old Beaver had bidden them. They arrived outside the estufa [kiva] and stopped. The Snakes inside the estufa heard someone walking outside. One of them was sent out of the estufa to look. Entering the estufa again, he said: "There are two little ones standing outside." The leader said to him: "Let them come in then. Why do you not tell them to come in?" The Snake then went out again and told the Fawns to come into the estufa of the Snakes. "Come in, little ones," said the Snake to them. So they entered. When they went in, the whole estufa was full of Snakes. "Sit down, little ones. What do you come here for?" Then the little Fawns sat down. Having sat down they told the Snakes: "The Old Giantess felt our little kidneys every day and threatened to kill us, and as we were running away, Old Beaver carried us across the river and told us to come on this way. That is the reason that we have come here." "Very well," said the Snake leader. No sooner had he said thus than the Old Giantess was heard coming outside the estufa. Then she arrived, all sweating, at the roof door. From there she spoke out:

"Insider, are not my Fawns in there?" "Yes, here they are. Come in and get them." "No, bring them out to me." "Come in and get them," said the Snake to her. She finally started to climb down the ladder. As she entered, she had only one more step to make before reaching the floor of the estufa, when a Snake that was lying beneath the ladder began to sound his rattle. "'Uluwia,²⁰" said the Old Giantess as she was hanging, missing the steps, on her way back up. But finally she got outside. She started home. Frightened by all the sticks lying along the road that she stepped on, she came to her home.

Said the leader of the Snakes to the little Fawns: "Now, little ones, you must go to the mountains, where you belong, and there you must increase. When you, little boy, reach Pin'o'ai you must branch off toward Jicarita Mountain,²¹ and there you must bring forth. And you, little girl, must go northeast from there and bring forth there among the mountains." As the leader of the Snakes told them thus, they went. As they went on they said to each other: "Now we are going to be lonesome, alone in the mountains. Instead of sending us together, he has told us to be separated."

When they came to Pin'o'ai they bade farewell to each other there and then parted. The male Fawn went up toward Jicarita Mountain and the female Fawn went northeast. As the male Fawn went on alone he was tired out and sighed in his lonesomeness: "I wonder how my poor little sister is getting along. Instead of the Snakes sending us together they have parted us." Thus he said as he went. Also the female Fawn cried as she went along where she had been told to go: "Hoke, hoke, me, me,²²" she said, "I wonder how my older brother is getting along. Instead of the Snakes sending us together they have parted us."

When they arrived at their destinations, they brought forth there among the mountains. This is the reason that deer live there among those mountains.

You have a tail.

The Old Giant Steals the Elf and is Slain

Once upon a time the Elf dwelt at Jicarita Mountain. And the Old Giant dwelt at Pheppittha. Going every day to where the people lived, he caught the children. Putting them into his pack basket he took them to his home.

And once he went to Jicarita Mountain. On top of Jicarita Mountain he found the Elf. "What are you doing here?" "I am not doing anything," the Elf said. "Well, get into my basket." "Why?" "Get into my basket, I said to you. If you do not get in I will take you and put you in." Then he took him and put him into the basket. Then the Old Giant headed for home. The Elf sang in the basket:

NO. 3. SONG OF THE ELF AS HE PACKED ALONG[23]

Me - 'e ye - he ye - he - he 'A - 'a - ha - a - ha - ha

'O - wi - t'a - i - nạ - lə - 'e - pa Ta - so - 'ĕl - hu tca - mẹn - nọ sạ.

"Do not move so much. You are very heavy." The Old Giant was going along all sweating.

When he brought the Elf to his home, the Old Giant was tired out, and lay down to take a nap. Then the Elf came out and found a pile of bones. He had a medicine bag tied on his person, and took the medicine out and spit it on the bones. Then he told the bones: "Little children, get up!" Then he sent two of them to look for pitch. After they brought the pitch, they put pitch all over the Elf, and he turned the children again into bones.

The Elf went into the Old Giant's house. When the Old Giant woke up, he fixed the fire. "Let me see; come this way, little one," he said to the Elf. The Giant said as he looked at him: "To-night I shall have a feast. This must be a very fat child." And he put him in the fire to roast. The Elf, spitting on the fire, entered the fire. Then he sang:

NO. 4. SONG OF THE ELF IN THE FIRE[24]

Transcription by Helen H. Roberts.

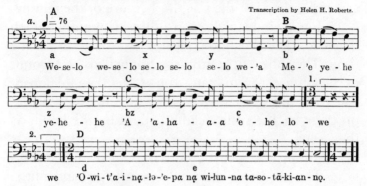

a.

We-se-lo we-se-lo se-lo se-lo se-lo we-'a Me-'e ye-he ye-he - he 'A-'a-ha - a-a 'e-he-lo-we we 'O-wi-t'a-i-nǫ-lə-'e-pa nǫ wi-lun-na tǫ-so-tǎ-ki-an-nǫ.

"I did not know that this child is indeed a singer."
Again the Old Giant went to sleep. While the Old Giant
was asleep, the Elf emerged from the fire, with sparks
flying. He took the poker stick and hit the Old Giant
on the head and killed him. Going outside and again
spitting on the bones, the children began to rise up.
Then the Elf told them: "Now I have killed for you the
Old Giant who has been eating you up. And now you
can go home without fear to where in your homes your
poor parents are thinking about you. I also live far away.
Also in my home my grandmother is thinking about
me. And I also am going thither. So I will bid you
good-by. You must go home." Then the children
thanked the Elf. They all started out.

This is why there are no more giants.

THE FAMINE

Long ago the people were dwelling at Picurís
Pueblo. And once there was a famine. The fields were

all bare. The people were suffering with hunger. A few at a time, they left the pueblo, because of the famine. Carrying their blankets and other belongings which they had, they began to go forth, two to five or six at a time. They all went southwest. Some fled, on account of the famine, to San Juan, Santa Clara, San Ildefonso. The men and women were some carrying their babies on their backs, some leading them by the hand, as they went.

Among those that went last were a man and his wife. They had two children — a little girl and a little boy. Having put their children to sleep, they carried away their household goods. Leaving their children sleeping, they went with the rest of the people.

When the children woke up, the mother and father were nowhere around. As the girl was only four years old and the boy six, they got up from where they were lying and began to cry. When they went up on the roof of their house, there was not a person around the village, not one to be seen. They got hungry and the little girl went down to the field and got some greens, and the little boy went down and got some kindlings. They built a fire, boiled the greens, and ate. In this way they subsisted for a long time. As the little boy slowly grew, he went out hunting and brought mice, birds, and chipmunks. Thus they subsisted. As he grew older, going out farther into the woods, he brought home rabbits, squirrels, and jackrabbits that he killed with his bow and arrows. As the years went by and as he grew stronger to shoot, he went up to the mountains to hunt and brought deer. Thus subsisting they dwelt.

The little girl had two Dolls. Every day she took

them out of a hole in the wall and played with them. One day the Dolls said: "These two poor children have been living in this way. To-morrow we will go down southeast below the Pueblo to where Shell Hat[25] lives, to supplicate him. Perhaps he may give us something"

The next day the Dolls came forth from the hole in the wall and went down below the Pueblo to Shell Hat's estufa [kiva]. When they arrived there they stopped outside Shell Hat's estufa. There were two macaw birds seated, one at each side of the roof-hole. They spread their wings and acted as if they were going to fly. "I wonder why they are fluttering their wings so. You go out to see," said Shell Hat to his son. When his son went outside the estufa and looked, there stood the Dolls at the roof-hole. He went back again into the estufa and said: "There are two little children standing outside." "Tell them to come in. Why do not you tell them to come in?" The Dolls were told to come in, and they entered.

As they entered they saw that the estufa was all made of shell. There was shell floor, shell ceiling, and all of the estufa was of shell. And there in his estufa was Shell Hat, all dressed in shell. He had a shirt of shell, a hat of shell, leggings of shell, earrings of shell. "What is the matter, little children, that you come to my sacred precinct? No one comes here, not even a little bird," said Shell Hat to them, lighting his pipe of shell as he told them thus. "Yes, we have come here to your sacred precinct because two poor little children who are keeping us have no food to eat. The little girl goes out to pick greens and the little boy goes out to hunt and kills whatever he can. That is the way that they have been subsisting, their parents having left them. That is why we have come down here to make a plea," the Dolls said to Shell Hat. "Well, so it is," said Shell Hat. As he said thus he entered a room and brought out with him five grains of corn — white, black, yellow, blue, and gray — and also white, black, and red beans. And he gave them to them, saying: "You must tell the little children to put these in a dark room. After they have put them in there they must lock the door tight. They must not look in there for four days. They must open it on the fourth day." As the Dolls were told thus, they sat there thanking Shell Hat.

The little girl looked for her two little Dolls in the wall hole, but did not find them. She looked all around the house, crying, but could not find them. But they entered the house again all of a sudden and had with them what Shell Hat had given them. "We have been down below the Pueblo where Shell Hat lives, and he has sent you these. He said that you must put these in a dark room, but you must not look in there for four days. You must look on the fifth day." When the children were told thus, they placed the corn and beans in a dark room.

The night of the fourth day the children could hardly sleep. The next morning as the sun was rising they got up and entered the room in which the corn and beans were. It was filled clear to the ceiling with corn of various colors, and white, black, and red beans. From that time on they cooked the way they wanted to and lived well.

One day one of the Picurís men who had gone to Santa Clara said to his wife: "I wonder if those two children that were left at the Pueblo are still living or not. Suppose I go and see." So saying, he started out. As he went along, he came to Paxenna. As the children sat on top of their house looking, they saw him

42

Threshing with goats. Picuris Pueblo, ca. 1905. Photo by Ed Andrews. Courtesy Museum of New Mexico, Neg. No. 15123.

and said: "Down southwest somebody is coming." As they watched the man coming, he came up to where they were sitting. They all wept as they shook hands with each other, and food was set out for him, and he ate. He slept there with them that night, and the next morning they sent him back to Santa Clara and to the other places where the people of Picurís were staying. The man went back and, calling all the people, told them to go back to the Pueblo. The people put what utensils they had on their backs and started for the Pueblo again.

When they arrived at the Pueblo the children shook hands with them and told them to come into their house. And their mother and father, packing things on their backs, also arrived. But their own children would not speak to them, nor did they tell them to come in. As they stood around there they finally put their packs on their backs and went toward the east. But whatever became of them or where they went to, nobody knew.

From that time on, it being spring, the Picurís people planted, and food was plentiful. Thenceforth they lived nicely. So this is the reason that the people at Picurís still plant and dwell, subsisting as well as they can.

You have a tail.

THE TWO DOVE MAIDEN SISTERS AND THE DROUTH

Once upon a time there lived two little Doves at the Pueblo of Picurís. Some of the Picurís youths at the Pueblo made their living by going out hunting every day to the mountains, and returned in the evening packing deer. And the two little Doves did nothing but plant every year. They lived, planting corn and beans of various colors in the spring, eating well and not thinking of hunting as the youths of Picurís did. They were seen every day early before sunrise in their fields where their crops were, having their hoes with them, singing.

One year they planted much corn and beans, but as the year was dry and there was no rain, their crops were drying up and they did not know what to do. Sometimes they would sit in the shade of a cottonwood tree all day, and the Picurís youths would look at them and would say to them: "These two little Doves are doing nothing but stay in the shade while their crops are drying up."

As the two little Doves did not like to have the Picurís youths talk to them thus, one day one of the Doves said: "I believe we will call the Buzzard; perhaps he can call the rain for us." Then they called the Buzzard. In a little while the Buzzard came to them. The Buzzard said to them: "Little ones, why do you bother me while I am having such a good time out in the heat?" Then the little Doves said: "We have called you, thinking you might be able to summon the rain for us, for our poor crops are drying up, and the Picurís youths tell us that we do nothing but just sit in the shade." Then the Buzzard said to them: "I do not like the rain, for the Sun is my father, so that is why I am going to take part on his side." As the Buzzard said thus, he flew away. "That old bald-headed Buzzard, let him go," said the two little Doves.

"Now we will call the Crow." So then they called the Crow. In a little while the Crow came to them. "Why, little ones, do you disturb me here from the mountains where I have been sitting in the shade so nicely?" said the Crow to them. The two little Doves said: "We have called you, thinking that you might be able to summon the rain for us, for our crops are drying up. And the Picurís youths are saying to us, because we sit in the shade, that we are lazy, that we are doing nothing but sit in the shade all day." As they said thus to the Crow, said the Crow: "I am satisfied sitting in the shade in the mountains; if I should call the rain, my wings would get wet and I would not be able to fly; As he said thus, the Crow flew away to the mountains. "That old lazy Crow, let him go where he wants to," said the two little Doves, and sadly they went to their house. "To-night we will go down to the river to bathe, and early to-morrow morning we will go to the top of Morning Mountain, for the Morning Star Boy lives there, and he might be able to help us."

That night they went down to the river to bathe, and started off early the next morning to Morning Mountain. When they reached there, they entered the estufa [kiva] of the Morning Star. "Why, little ones, do you come to my estufa? Now I am going to eat you up." Then the two little Doves told the Morning Star: "We have come here to see if you could call the rain for us, for our poor crops are drying up." "Very well," said the Morning Star to them, "to-day I will call the rain for you, little ones. Do not be sad about it." When they were told thus, they went back home again. As they were reaching home, a few drops of rain began to fall. Then in a little while it rained hard. They went over to where their corn was growing. There they were drenched, but were feeling happy as they walked about. And they said: "These crops that we have we will give away to the Picurís people, so that they will not do so much hunting, so that they may learn to work." As they said thus, spreading their wings out they both flew away. From that time the Picurís people lived cultivating the crops of the two little Doves.

So this is the reason that the people of Picurís grow crops every year, because they were given them by the two little Doves.

The Two Dove Maiden Sisters Who Became Stars

Once upon a time the people dwelt at Picurís. And two Dove Maidens dwelt there with their grandmother. The Picurís maidens were grinding corn and were going about with their faces all powdered up. The Dove Maidens and their grandmother did nothing but make baskets.

Once they told their grandmother: "Grandmother, why do we not grind corn like the rest of the Picurís maidens? With their faces all powdered up, they are going about outside. And we do nothing but make baskets." "My dear children," said the grandmother, "you must not say that." "To-night get the corn ready, for we are going to grind in the morning," said the Dove Maidens to their grandmother. When it got evening, the grandmother, weeping, took out the tinaja and toasted some corn.

The next morning the Dove Maidens got ready to grind. Pouring the corn on the metate, they ground. And they sang:

NO. 5. SONG OF THE DOVE MAIDEN SISTERS
AS THEY BECOME STARS[26]

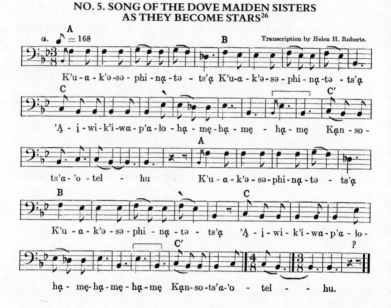

As they ground, they rose slowly higher and higher. Their poor grandmother sat weeping. Said she: "My dear children, you must not do thus. Stop grinding!" The Dove Maidens did not listen. Singing, they ground. They rose slowly higher. Their grandmother sat weeping. They reached the ceiling. They rose slowly higher. "My dear children," their grandmother said, "you must not do thus. Come back here!" The Dove Maidens disappeared. They are the two little stars above Jicarita Mountain.

This is the reason that it is well to obey one's parents, and this is the reason that Makiuto and Potoke[27] are above Jicarita Mountain.

You have a tail.

The Woman and the Wolf

Once upon a time the people were dwelling at Picurís. The women, after it got dark, were to remain inside their houses.

And one woman in the night had no water. She took the water jar and went down to Painon to get water. As she was pouring the water with her gourd, a Wolf came to her. "What are you doing?" he said. "I am pouring water," the woman said to the Wolf. "Get on my back, then," the Wolf said to her. "I am already about to take the water to my house," said the woman. "Get on my back, I said to you, or I will eat you up right here." The woman got afraid, left the water jar, and got on the Wolf's back.

And the Wolf took the woman up to the mountains. When he had brought her to the mountain top, the Wolf went northeast, northwest, southwest, and southeast,[28] to call the other wolves. The woman then climbed a tall pinyon tree.

Her husband, when his wife did not come up from below quickly, yelled as a signal from the top of the house. And shortly men with their weapons arrived.

When the Old Wolf arrived from his summoning [the other wolves], the woman was sitting in the top of the pinyon tree.

The men all gathered for search. And then at about midnight one man found the woman. Then the man gave a yell. After the rest came they took the woman home again. The woman was scolded very much by the men. And this is why the women, after it gets dark, do not go forth from inside the houses alone, for something might happen to them.

THE ANTS

Once upon a time at Komaithotha ["Needle Horn Pile"] dwelt the Ants. [29] No birds came around there, and so they lived without fear. They went wherever they pleased without fear, for there was not even a little Hummingbird around near where they lived.

One day their leader told them at a meeting: "My people, in four days from to-day we are going to dance here in this land of ours; we will entertain the other people. So you must be looking for such things as red paint, beads, war bonnets, and whatever dress you may need. And we will call the flying animals of all kinds here to look on." As their leader instructed them thus, they said: "It seems all right the way you say, we will get ready to dance four days from to-day." And the Ants were getting ready within that time. They went around borrowing things from their neighbors whom they knew.

On the fourth day the leader assembled them in their estufa [kiva]. And they then were told: "My people, to-morrow the day arrives on which we are to dance, so the flying animals of every kind are to come here to our home to look on. And so you must all do your best."

The next morning as the sun was rising the Ants gathered in their estufa. After they were all assembled, both men and women, all dressed up nicely, emerged from the estufa. When they looked around at the trees, there were birds of every kind sitting there.

They were only dancing a little while when all the Eagles, who were sitting looking on, flew to the ground where the Ants were dancing, and being hungry, began to eat the Ants up. After they had enough, they flew away to their homes. The leader of the Ants said to the people: "Dance your best, my people, for there are many people looking on."

When he had hardly finished saying thus, the Redtail Hawks, from where they were sitting looking on, flew down to where the Ants were dancing, and began to eat up the Ants. When they got enough, they all flew away to their homes. The leader of the Ants said to them: "My people, dance your best, for there are many people looking on."

When he had hardly finished saying thus, the Buzzards, from where they were sitting looking on, flew down to where the Ants were dancing, and began to eat the Ants. When they got enough, they all flew away to their homes. By that time there were very few of the Ants left, but they would not quit dancing. They danced all the more. Their leader said to them: "My people, dance your best, for there are still many people looking on."

When he had hardly finished saying thus, the Turkeys, from where they were sitting looking on, flew down to where the Ants were dancing, and began to eat the Ants up. When they got enough, they all flew away to their homes. By that time there were but few of the Ants left. But they danced their best. Their leader said to them: "My people, dance your best, for there are still many people who are looking on."

When he had hardly finished saying thus, the Bluebirds, from where they were sitting in the trees looking on, flew down to where the Ants were dancing, and ate the Ants that were left, together with their leader. And then the Bluebirds all flew away to their homes.

And the other birds who were looking on flew

away. Because there were no more Ants left for them, they all said: "Since the other birds have not left us any Ants, let us also go and look for some." When the birds who were sitting looking on said thus, they all scattered to look for Ants.

So this is the reason that the birds to-day hunt around for ants, and also the reason that birds like ants, because they ate the ants at that time.

THE SANDHILL CRANES

Once there lived a flock of Sandhill Cranes up in the clouds in the sky. And they drank the water from the clouds, and also built their nests upon the clouds, and lived well. Once their leader said to them: "I believe we will go down to the earth. The earth has many rivers in every direction. And in the water fishes, frogs, and other water animals are living. And there are also many trees where we could build our nests. When we reach the earth, going to where the rivers are, we can live well, eating nicely and getting fat." As their leader told them thus, all of the Sandhill Cranes agreed. Then they said to their leader: "All that you have said about the earth seems to be very good. So we all want to go to the earth." As they said thus, they all flew toward the earth.

As they flew down from the clouds they lighted at P'axwi'oxwal Spring. And they lived, eating well, eating fishes and frogs every day. But the Sandhill Cranes, as they drank so much water, soon drank all of the water from the spring, together with the fishes and frogs. "We will fly to another river, as this spring does not hold enough water," their leader said to them.

Then they flew to the spring of Jicarita Mountain. When they arrived they lighted at the spring. At the spring they lived, catching fishes, frogs, and other water animals that lived there, and drinking the water of the spring. There they lived for a while, eating well and drinking as much as they wanted. But they soon drank all the water from the spring, together with the fishes and frogs. Then their leader said to them: "Now we will fly northwest to where the Taos River [Pueblo Creek] lies, for this spring does not contain enough water."

As their leader told them thus, they flew northwest to the Taos River. When they reached there they lighted near the river. And they lived a while by the river, catching fishes, frogs and other water animals that lived in the river, eating well and drinking much. As they drank so much, in a short time drinking up all the water of the Northwest River,[30] together with the fishes and frogs and whatever else lived in the river, their leader said to them: "Now we will fly to the river of Picurís village. There there may be more water. This Taos River does not contain enough water."

As their leader told them thus, they flew to the Picurís village. When they reached there they lighted by the river. And they lived well for a while, catching fishes, frogs, and whatever other water animals lived there in the water. But living there for a while they soon drank up all the water, together with the fishes, frogs, and other water animals that lived there. "Now we will fly to the Rio Grande,[31] for this Picurís River does not contain enough water, and like nothing we have drunk up all the water, fishes, frogs, and other water animals."

As their leader told them thus, they flew to the Rio Grande. When they reached the Rio Grande they lighted near the river. They drank the water of the Rio Grande and ate the fishes, frogs, and other water animals that lived there, and lived well. All the Sandhill Cranes did their very best to drink up the water, but could not finish drinking the water of the Rio Grande, neither could they finish eating up the Rio Grande fishes, frogs, and other water animals that lived there. "This river must be very strong, so here we will make our headquarters, here we will build our nests and increase in number." When their leader told them thus, they made their homes there.

So this is the reason that there are Sandhill Cranes living on the Rio Grande, because there is plenty of water.

A BABY IS STOLEN BY AN OWL

Once there lived people at the Pueblo. And there also dwelt there a certain woman who had a baby that cried a great deal. As the baby cried every night, the mother did not know what to do with it. Soothing songs were sung to it, but the baby would not stop crying. It cried day and night, and one day the mother took the baby out upon the roof and left it there.

As the child cried continually on the roof, it was heard by an Owl. The Owl came flying to where the baby was crying and picked it up in his claws and carried it to Paxeputa, up on some very high rocks where the Owl dwelt. When he brought the baby to his home, he laid it on a flat rock. Every day the Owl would feed the baby whatever he could, and the baby stayed there several days.

One evening a man was coming home from hunting from the northeast, and as he was passing along the trail opposite the Owl's home, he heard a baby cry. There he stood to listen for a while. The baby sounded crying up on the top of the rock. "I believe I will go up toward where the baby sounds crying and see." As he said thus, he climbed to the top of the rocks. When he reached the top, the baby sat on the rock, crying. He took it, put it on his back, and carried it home.

When he reached home, he took the baby over to where its mother lived. He handed the child to its mother and scolded her, telling her: "Why do you leave the baby outside, crying? I found it at the home of the Owl this evening as I was returning home from hunting. I brought it from there. If it were not for me, your child could have been eaten by the Owl." As the man said thus to the woman, he went home.

So this is the reason that the women at Pueblo no longer leave their babies crying outside alone, lest the Owls might take the babies to their homes.

THE SPHYNX MOTH AND THE OLD COYOTE

There once lived at Picurís Pueblo a Sphynx Moth and his grandmother. The Sphynx Moth was a great believer; he believed everything concerning the customs of the people. And he was very obedient to his grandmother; he would go wherever his grandmother would tell him, without talking back.

Once his grandmother said to him: "My grandson, you must make plumeros [Spanish: feather bunches] to-night and take them to Kan'in'ai ["At the Buffalo Track"], to the southeast, early to-morrow morning. The Picurís youths and even Picurís maidens take their plumeros there and supplicate. So early to-morrow morning you must carry these plumeros and go there to supplicate." So that night the Sphynx Moth made plumeros the way his grandmother had told him.

Early the next morning, carrying the plumeros, he set out for Kan'in'ai, to the southeast. As he went along through the fields, he met Old Coyote, who was hunting around. "Good morning, where are you going?" the Old Coyote said to the Sphynx Moth. "I am going over southeast to Kan'in'ai," said the Sphynx Moth. "What is it that you are carrying?" said the Old Coyote to the Sphynx Moth. Then the Sphynx Moth said: "I am carrying my dead grandmother over southeast to Kan'in'ai." Then the Old Coyote said: "Then wait here for me, for I am going to get my grandmother."

As Old Coyote told the Sphynx Moth thus, he ran toward Tciuthotha ["Eagle Pile Mountain"] where his own grandmother was. When he arrived there he hunted for a bag and went inside the house where his grandmother was toasting corn meal. And he said to his grandmother: "Grandmother, get into this bag!" But the grandmother would not get into it. "Get in here, I tell you," said Old Coyote to his grandmother. But his grandmother would not get in. The Old Coyote said: "If you do not get in, I will hit you on the head with a fire poker and then put you in this bag." The Old Coyote told his grandmother thus several times, but he soon got disgusted and, taking the fire poker which was lying by the fireplace, he struck his grandmother, where she was sitting toasting the corn meal, and then putting her into the bag and carrying her, he brought his grandmother over to where the Sphynx Moth was waiting for him. "Now we shall both take our grandmothers over southeast to Kan'in'ai," said the Old Coyote to the Sphynx Moth. The Sphynx Moth assented.

Then they both started off to Kan'in'ai, to the southeast. As they went along talking on the road they reached Kan'in'ai. There in a rocky place the Sphynx Moth dug, and laid his plumeros. When the Old Coyote noticed what the Sphynx Moth was doing, he discovered that instead of a dead grandmother it was plumeros that he was laying under a rock. And the Old Coyote said to himself: "This Sphynx Moth has told me a lie. Instead of having a dead grandmother in his bag, he is putting the plumeros under the rock. Now, I will go over there where he is and bite him." As the Sphynx Moth heard him saying thus, he flew away. Then the Old Coyote was very angry, and he said to himself: "That accursed Sphynx Moth, it is on account of him that I have killed my grandmother." As the Sphynx Moth disappeared as soon as he flew, the Old Coyote did not know what to do. Again he packed his grandmother on his back, and started for home. He was crying as he went along the road.

As he reached home, his children heard him crying from where they were playing, and said to each other: "But why is it that our father is so happy? He is coming along the road singing. Let us all go to meet him." As they said thus, the little Coyotes went to meet their father. When they met him, they asked him: "Our father, why are you so happy? Why are you coming along singing so loud?" Then their father told them: "My children, I am not coming along singing, but I am coming along crying. It is on account of that accursed Sphynx Moth that I have killed my grandmother by hitting her on the head, because he told me a lie. If I had known this, I would have bitten him while

I had a chance." As their father told the little Coyotes thus, they all joined crying. The Old Coyote carried his grandmother into the house and set her down again at the fireplace where she had sat toasting corn meal, and gave her the corn meal toasting sticks and told her, although she was dead: "Now, grandmother, finish toasting your corn meal!" As he would set her down she would topple over again, and at last the Old Coyote got more angry, and he took the fire poker and struck his grandmother again on the head, to be sure that she had been killed. Then he put her on his back and took her to the arroyo to bury her.

So this is the reason that coyotes nowadays are smart, because they learned this kind of work long ago; this is the reason that the coyotes are smarter than any other four-footed animal.

You have a tail.

KOYOWIXELAPAN FETCHES FIRE

Once upon a time the people were dwelling at Picurís. And there also lived Koyowixelapan[32] with her grandmother.

One time when they came home from going around wood-gathering, their fire had gone out. "You must go outside to look for fire," said Koyowixelapan's grandmother to her. Then Koyowixelapan went out to look for fire. There was a bright light down in the arroyo at Patopona'ai ["Under the Acqueduct-Log"]. "I believe I will go down where the bright light is to get fire," she said. Then she went down. When she arrived there, the Wizards were dancing inside the estufa [kiva], and they sang:

NO. 6. SONG OF THE WIZARDS AS KOYOWIXELAPAN ENTERS THEIR ESTUFA[33]

Transcription by Helen H. Roberts.

Koyowixelapan then went into the estufa [kiva]. As she went in, she was asked by the Wizards to join in the dance. She then joined in the dance.

Because she did not return soon, her grandmother began to get uneasy about her. She said: "But where did Koyowixelapan go? I believe I will got out and look for her," she said, and went out. As she went about searching, she went crying:

59

Ramita Martinez, potter. Picuris Pueblo, 1959. Photo by Mrs. John Champ. Courtesy Museum of New Mexico, Neg. No. 31057.

NO. 7. CRYING SONG OF THE GRANDMOTHER
AS SHE SEEKS KÓYOWIXELAPAN[34]

Ko - yo - wị - xə - ła - - pan   Ko - yo - wị - xə - ła -

pan   'Ai - wị - nọ - ke ha - yu - wi mẹ - hu   mẹ - hu.

She then went over to where the Wizards had their place all lighted up. When she arrived where they were dancing she called inside through the roof-hole: "Insider, is not my Koyowixelapan here?" She repeated this two or three times, but the Wizards would pay no attention to her. Koyowixelapan was dancing with them as they sang:

NO. 8. SONG OF THE WIZARDS AS THEY
MAKE KOYOWIXELAPAN AN OLD WOMAN[35]

Mi - ma - t'ā - la - pi - a - pọ   t'ā - ła - pi - a - pọ he - nai - 'a - ne - 'e - nạ

Mi - ma - t'ā - la - pi - a - pọ   he - nai - 'a - ne - 'e - nạ

Ha - na - ne - nạ he - nai - 'a - ne - 'e - nạ.   Mi - ma - t'ā - la - pi - a - pọ

t'ā - la - pi - a - pọ he - nai - 'a - ne - 'e - nạ   Mi - ma - t'ā - la - pi - a - pọ he -

nai - 'a - ne - 'e - nạ   Ha - na - ne - nạ he - nai - 'a - ne - 'e - nạ.

As they were dancing, the leader heard the voice of Koyowixelapan's grandmother, and told them to stop. As they were told thus, they stopped dancing. There at the roof hole Koyowixelapan's grandmother was heard saying: "Insider, is not my Koyowixelapan here?" "Yes, she is here. Come down and get her!" said the Wizards to her. "No, bring her out for me!" she said. Their leader said to them: "Take her out, for she, poor one, is now very old." When they brought her out, they both went to their home.

So this is the reason that the girls are not permitted to go out to look for fire in the evening, lest the Wizards might catch them.

You have a tail.

THE TURKEYS AND THE GREAT FLOOD

Once upon a time there lived some Turkeys at Ke'oma Mountain. And one time there came a certain bird to tell them that all four-footed and flying animals must go up Pueblo Peak, since the whole earth was to be covered by rain, it being that the Power was to send rain to the earth.

Then the day arrived for them to go. All the birds that lived at Ke'oma Mountain went to Pueblo Peak. And two Turkeys started to go there with their little brother, leading their little brother by the hand. As they got near, their little brother was growing tired and began to cry. "Keep on, our little brother," said his older brothers to him. As he grew tired he went along crying. "Do not cry, our little brother, we shall now soon reach Pueblo Peak," said his older brothers to him as they went along.

They finally came to the top of Pueblo Peak. When they reached the top, four-footed and flying animals of every kind were already there. Since it was raining hard, the water was almost reaching the top. Some of the birds were sitting on top of the trees and just as the water was about to reach to the top of Pueblo Peak it stopped raining.

So this is the reason why the Turkeys have their feathers white at the end of the tail, because they were touched by the foam of the water. And this is also the reason why some of the flying animals and four-footed animals are spotted, because as they ascended, fleeing from the rain, their feathers were touched by the foam of the water.

You have a tail.

The Origin of the Scalp House

Once upon a time people were living at the Pueblo. Also people were living up northwest at Taos. As the Picurís people were at war with the Taos, the people were all inside their houses without lights as soon as it got dark, for the Taos used to come around at night.

Now a certain Picurís man put his quiver on his back and took his bow and started off in the evening, before sunset, up northwest for where the Taos lived. When he arrived there he sat inside an old house, waiting for it to get dark. As he sat there waiting, and as it was getting dark, he heard the Taos children who were playing say: "Now we must go inside, for the Picurís might catch us."[36]

When it grew dark, he went into the first house he came to. There was only one woman there, who was holding a child in her arms. The man took out his sword and severed the woman's neck. He took the head and started up toward Picurís again. As he went along and came to Paxwinowia'ai[37] he turned and looked back, and torches were flashing around where the Taos lived. Some of the lights were coming along the roads by which he had come. The man ran his best toward Picurís. When he got out to Petcotheke'ai ["Above the Home of the Snakes"] he gave a war whoop. The men of Picurís, when they heard the war whoop, took the arrows, guns, and whatever weapons they had, and hurried toward the top of Petcotheke'ai Mountain. When they reached the top, they found the man with the head of the Taos woman. They built a fire at the top and had a war-dance.

When they finished dancing, they took the head down to the Pueblo. "Let us build a scalp house; we might happen to go to war and bring more scalps, and could hang them up," some of the men said. And so they built a scalp house the very next day.

So this is the reason that scalps which were brought by men who went to war are hanging at the Pueblo to this day.

THE SUNKEN ESTUFA

My children, long ago when I was a child like you at the Pueblo, my grandparents and even my parents used to tell me like this, that a long time ago, when at Picurís Pueblo they still used to carry on by native custom and do everything by ceremony, one spring the people were grinding flowers at Keppui. Even to this time you can see the place as you pass by, as it is sunken.

Winnowing wheat. Picuris Pueblo, ca. 1935. Photo by T. Harmon Parkhurst. Courtesy Museum of New Mexico, Neg. No. 3333.

Perhaps there may be some 250 people buried in that estufa [kiva]. Among those buried there are the men and women who were singing. The prettiest looking of all were the paiene (literally, "grinders"), whom they nowadays called kwel'ene (maidens). But these girls ground flowers long ago in ceremony, and that is why they were so called. I suppose that all the people that were in there were dressed up nicely.

So that is the reason, my children, that the old men at the Pueblo still talk about it, that one might get rich with beads, earrings, and many other things that are buried there. You know that our palefaced brothers value ancient articles much. If I were to have my own way and were to be permitted at the Pueblo, I would get some of the palefaces to help me dig that place; I would gladly go to dig that estufa. That is all I have to say to you about that estufa at the Pueblo, for that is all I know. So put the impression in your head as I have told you, so that when these old people have passed away you can take their place and have this story to tell.

The Old Coyote Woman and The Crow Visit Each Other

Once there dwelt a Crow[38] at Tauxatho'ai.[39] And the Old Coyote Woman together with her young ones dwelt at 'Q'ai ["At the Salt"]. Once the Old Coyote Woman said to her children: "To-morrow I am going for a visit to Tauxatho'ai, where my friend the Crow lives. And so do not expect me to return soon." The next day the Old Coyote Woman combed her hair and dressed up nicely, and then went for a visit to the home of the Crow.

When she arrived at the home of the Crow, she was told to come in. When the Old Coyote Woman went inside, the Crow's house was very beautiful. The floor was very sleek, like ice. As the Old Coyote Woman walked about on the floor, she could not keep her feet because it was so very sleek. As she rolled about she sat down and she and the Crow talked together. Then the Old Coyote Woman asked the Crow: "My friend, how did your floor get so sleek?" Then the Crow said: "I just brought some mud in, spread it on the floor, and then I rolled all over the floor, and thus my floor got sleek." Then the Old Coyote Woman said: "Very well, I too, when I go home this evening, will ask my children to make mud, and I will take it into the house and I will roll, so that my floor will get as sleek as yours."

As they sat there talking thus, the Old Coyote Woman said: "We ought to have something to eat while visiting." "Quite so, bring me over that fire poker lying by the fireplace," said the Crow to the Old Coyote Woman. The Old Coyote Woman brought the fire poker to the Crow, and she began to whip herself on the nose. As she whipped herself on the nose, a quantity of pinyon nuts dropped out of her nose. After she had filled a basket with pinyon nuts she set it for the Old Coyote Woman to eat. As the Old Coyote Woman was voracious, she ate the pinyon nuts shell and all. In the evening the Old Coyote Woman said: "Now I must be going home. To-morrow evening you must come over for a visit to my house." Then the Old Coyote Woman went back to her home.

When she reached home she told her children: "My children, the floor of my friend the Crow is so sleek that I could not keep my feet. So I too am going to make my floor smooth like that. So you make mud outdoors right now, since the Crow is coming here for a visit to-morrow evening. I want her to find my floor as sleek as hers." The little Coyotes started to work making mud. When they finished the mud, they carried it inside and spread it on the floor. When they had finished spreading it, the Old Coyote Woman started to roll. All muddy, she rolled around, but it did not get sleek at all. The floor was imprinted with her large claws. "Now I will surprise the Crow. My floor is just as sleek as hers."

So the next evening the Crow went to the Old Coyote Woman's home for a visit. When she arrived the Old Coyote Woman said to her: "Come in! Come in! Just look at my floor!" As the Crow entered and saw the floor, there were large and plain imprints of the claws, the ears, the tail, the hips, the teeth of the Old Coyote Woman. The Crow made herself fall, just for fun, and said: "Old Coyote Woman, how did it happen that your floor got so sleek?" Then the Old Coyote Woman told her: "Just by rolling over and over." Then they both sat down together to talk.

After they sat talking a while, the Crow said to the Old Coyote Woman: "Old Coyote Woman, we ought to have something to eat while visiting." Then the Old Coyote Woman said: "Very well, bring me over that fire poker which is lying by the fireplace." Then the Crow brought the fire poker and the Old Coyote Woman began to whip herself with it on the nose. As she whipped herself on the nose, it began to bleed, instead of pinyon nuts coming out. "Whip yourself harder," said the Crow to her. Then the Old Coyote Woman began to whip herself harder. Then her nose began to bleed more. But she would not stop whipping herself on the nose. Finally the Old Coyote Woman killed herself by whipping herself on the nose. As she lay dead, the Crow said, laughing: "The thus easily fooled Old Coyote Woman thought that she would do the same as I." As the Crow said thus, she ate the Old Coyote Woman's eyeballs, and then flew away.

So this is the reason that crows are fond of eyeballs. You have a tail.

Old Coyote Woman, Jackrabbit, and Bluejay Grind Together

Once upon a time there lived at Kepui a Jackrabbit and a Bluejay. Once they said to each other: "Tomorrow let us grind." So the next morning they put their shelled corn on their metates and began to grind. The Jackrabbit sang as she ground:

NO. 9. THE JACKRABBIT'S GRINDING SONG[40]

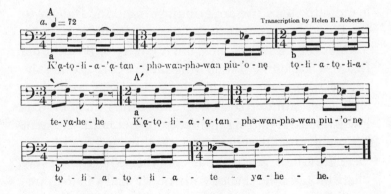

Also the Bluejay sang as she ground:

NO. 10. THE BLUEJAY'S GRINDING SONG[41]

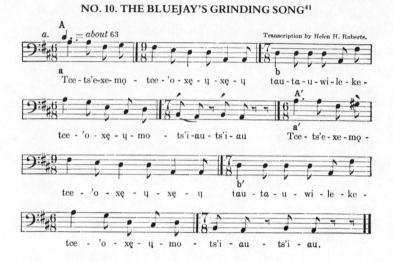

Then Old Coyote Woman, who was hunting around there, heard the song. "But where must this beautiful singing be coming from? I believe I will go to where it sounds from." As she said thus, she went over to where it sounded from. When she arrived where the Jackrabbit and the Bluejay were grinding, she said: "Are you grinding?" "Yes, we are grinding," said the Bluejay to her, "go and get your shelled corn and join us."

As they told her thus, she went up to Tciuthoma ["at the Eagle Pile"] to get the shelled corn. When she reached home she went to where there were cedar trees and picked some cedar berries and putting them in shallow basket and putting the basket on her head, she went hurrying along to where the Jackrabbit and the Bluejay were grinding. When she arrived there she said: "Now I have brought the shelled corn; now I shall join in grinding." When the Jackrabbit and the Bluejay saw the shallow basket of cedar berries, they said to the Coyote: "We do not grind cedar berries here on our metates, because it makes the metates look brown and it will not come off." As they told her thus, she went outside again and threw the cedar berries away and went back to Tciuthoma.

When she arrived home she put the best shelled corn that she had in the basket, put it on her head, and again went hurrying along to where the Jackrabbit and the Bluejay were grinding. When she arrived there, the Jackrabbit said to her: "Now you may grind; that shelled corn that you have is very good." As the Old Coyote Woman was told thus, she put the shelled corn on a metate and the three of them ground.

As they ground, the Jackrabbit said to the Old Coyote Woman: "This time let us grind with all our strength to see who is the strongest to grind. So we will close our eyes and grind." The Old Coyote Woman said: "Very well." Then they all started to grind with all their might. As the Old Coyote Woman was grinding with all her might, the Jackrabbit and the Bluejay hit her on the head with their handstones, as she was grinding in the middle, and killed her.

So that is the reason that people grind.

THE OLD COYOTE AND THE THREE GOURDS

Long ago three Gourds were living at Kepui. Once they came out of their hole to bask. As they sat basking, Old Coyote also came out of his hole to bask just opposite. "Let us call the Old Coyote names; if he should come after us, we will flee into our hole," said the Gourds. So they started to call Old Coyote names, from where they were basking. "Old Coyote, unsuccessful hunter, wet worn-out moccasins, pitch mouth!"

As the Old Coyote heard the Gourds from where he was basking, he said to them: "If you keep calling me names I will go over there and bite every one of you." "Old Coyote, unsuccessful hunter, wet worn-out moccasins, pitch mouth!" said the Gourds. "Shut up! If you keep calling me that, I will go over there and bite every one of you." But the Gourds would not listen to Old Coyote. "Old Coyote, unsuccessful hunter, wet worn-out moccasins, pitch mouth!" said the Gourds to him. Finally the Old Coyote got real mad and went after them where they were basking. Then the Gourds fled into their hole.

Then the Old Coyote began to dig into the hole. As he dug he reached one of the Gourds. "Who was it that called me 'Old Coyote, unsuccessful hunter, wet worn-out moccasins, pitch mouth?'" the Old Coyote asked the Gourd. "One that is below," said the Gourd. As he said thus, away he fled.

As the Old Coyote dug he reached another Gourd. "Who was it that called me 'Old Coyote, unsuccessful hunter, wet worn-out moccasins, pitch mouth?'" the Old Coyote asked the Gourd. "One that is below," said the Gourd. As he said thus, away he fled.

As the Old Coyote dug he reached the last Gourd that was in the hole. "Who was it that called me 'Old Coyote, unsuccessful hunter, wet worn-out moccasins, pitch mouth?'" the Old coyote asked the Gourd. "One that is below," said the Gourd. As he said thus, away he fled.

The Old Coyote, again digging, found a stone that look like a Gourd. "Who was it that called me 'Old Coyote, unsuccessful hunter, wet worn-out moccasins, pitch mouth?'" the Old Coyote asked the stone. As the stone had no life in it, it lay without speaking. Again the Old Coyote asked the stone: "Who was it that called me 'Old Coyote, unsuccessful hunter, wet worn-out moccasins, pitch mouth?'" As the stone had no life in it, it lay without speaking. "Why do you not answer me? I will bite you here on the spot," said the Old Coyote to the stone. But the stone lay there and said nothing. The Old Coyote asked the same question several times. As it could not answer, the Old Coyote grew angry and bit the stone, thinking it was a Gourd. He then broke all his teeth. He sat there a while, crying from the ache of his teeth, and went home.

So this is the reason that the coyotes do not bite gourds any more.

THE CRICKET AND THE COYOTE

Once upon a time the Cricket dwelt southeast at Kan'in'ai ["at the Buffalo Tracks"] and the Coyote dwelt at Tcuxwetho'ai ["at Eagle Tail Pile"]. One day the Coyote said to himself: "I think to-day I will go for a walk down southeast to Kan'in'ai to see what I can find there."

Early in the morning he ate his breakfast and then went to Kan'in'ai. Then arriving at Kan'in'ai he came to where the Cricket was lying basking beside the road. As he passed there, he stepped on the Cricket. The Cricket said to the Coyote: "Why do you not speak?" The Coyote said: "I do not speak to such looking people as that." "Very well," said the Cricket, "we will make a bet then to see whose people are the strongest." "Very well," said the Coyote to the Cricket, "we will meet to-morrow then down by the river." "Very well," said the cricket, "we shall see each other again to-morrow." Then the Coyote went home.

That night the Cricket called his people. All the Bumble Bees, White-striped Bees, Honey Bees, and other winged stingers he called. And the Coyote was doing the same. That night he called all the four-footed animals that live in the mountains — the Wolves, the Mountain lions, the Wildcats, the Bears, and other beasts of prey that there are.

The next day as the sun was rising the Coyote's people began to come. After all of them had arrived he said to them: "My people, over southeast at Kan'in'ai, where I went for a walk yesterday, the Cricket asked me to bet. That is why I am calling you to-day." "Very well," said the other beasts of prey, "we will show the Cricket to-day." Then the Coyote started ahead of the rest, and they went to Kan'in'ai.

When they came to the Picurís River, the Coyote said. "Wait here. I am going across the river to see the Cricket." He then went across the river. Arriving at the Cricket's home, the Cricket was already waiting for him. "Are you ready?" said the Coyote to the Cricket. "Yes, I am ready," said the Cricket; "you are to send your best man here." "Very well," said the Coyote, and then went back across the river to where his people were waiting. "Very well," said the Coyote to his people, "I will go over first, to see what is going to happen to me." Then he went across. When he arrived at the Cricket's home, the Cricket turned all the Bees loose on him. He was stung by the Bees in his eyes, ears, mouth, and all over his body. He bit some of them, but that did not help him any. When he came to the river he plunged into the water and dived, but when he emerged the Bees stung him again. At last he arrived where his people were waiting, and said: "The Cricket's people are well supplied with weapons."

"Very well, I will go this time," said the Mountain lion. Then he went. When he arrived at the home of the Cricket, all the Bees were turned loose again. He was stung the way the Coyote had been, in the eyes, ears, mouth, and all over his body. The Mountain lion bit some of them and hit others with his paws, and ran toward the river. When he arrived at the river, he plunged in. When he emerged from the water the Bees stung him again. When he came out of the water he went to where his people were waiting and said to his people: "My people, the Cricket has defeated us. His people are stronger. Although I have many teeth, although I have many claws, I did not last very long among the Bees. And so now, my people, you must go to your homes. Do not go over to where the Bees live. You must go to your homes." As the Mountain lion told them thus, they all went to their homes.

And this is why it hurts when bees sting you.

You have a tail.

Mission of San Lorenzo at Picuris Pueblo, ca. 1915. Photo by Carter H. Harrison. Courtesy Museum of New Mexico, Neg. No. 3335.

Folkways

Collected by John P. Harrington
from Rosendo Vargas

Birth Customs

When a woman of Picurís bears a child whoever cuts the child's navel cord names the child. While the child is being named, a string is tied to its wrist. And then it is laid where its mother is lying. An ear of yellow corn is laid beside the child. This ear of corn becomes the child's mother for 30 days. The woman does not get up for 30 days after she gives birth to the child, but lies along with her child. And during this time she drinks only warm water, and food is made for her apart.

At the end of the 30 days the woman gets up from her lying and dresses up nicely and makes an excursion to the top of Thepiapittha ["Morning Mountain"]. She takes along sacred meal to give to the fetishes there, and arriving there she prays for her child. If the child is a girl, the mother prays that she may grind, cook, and do well the other kinds of work that women do. And if the child is a boy, she prays that he may be brave, a hunter, a runner, and do well the other kinds of work that men do. Then the mother goes back to her house. And then the ear of corn which lay as a mother by the side of the child is taken out of there and thrown away. From then on the ear of corn is no longer the child's mother; from then on the woman who bore the child is the real mother.

Thus the Picurís women bear children.

Death Customs

When the people of the Pueblo are sick they are doctored by native medicine men. Nowadays the Indian medicine men are not as active as they used to be long ago, since the white doctors have come more among the people. But at times the Indian medicine men still perform their ceremonies. Since the people of the Pueblo are all Christians, if they should get very sick and think that they are going to die, they usually send for the priest at Peñasco; and when the priest arrives at the home of the sick person, the sick person confesses to the priest. But still some of the Indians sing their medicine songs to a sick person for his recovery. When a person is dying, or even already dead, or whenever they can get around to it, the people make a plumero for him, giving it into his hands, and put a strip of black mica on his face, and then a death song is sung to him. It is called "making the road song." This song is sung to him so that the road will lead him southwest toward where the sun sets.

When they finish singing this song to him, he is laid face up and is told to drink water. The people one at a time pour water into a pottery dish, dipping two fingers in, and then put a few drops at a time into the dead person's mouth, each time representing different springs of the mountains about the Pueblo. As the water is put into the dead person's mouth, they name one spring each time, saying: "Drink from such and such a spring!" After all the people who are present there have told him to drink the water, he is then laid, face up, in the middle of the floor, and is left there according to the custom of the Catholics. As the person lies during the night in the middle of the floor, candles are lighted on both sides of where he is lying. All of his relatives, men and women, that are there, sing Christian hymns all through the night.

And the next morning as he is taken out for burial, a bag of lunch is tied on his side, of the food that he used to like. Then, before he is carried from where he is lying, a man who is no kin to him comes in with cedar sprigs, and as the dead person is taken from where he is lying, the man with the cedar sprigs pretends that he is sweeping out death, singing a sacred song softly as he goes outside. From there he goes southwest for about 2 miles to throw death away toward where the sun sets. The people of the Pueblo believe that all the people who die go southwest, toward where the sun sets, to live. This ceremony is called the throwing away of death. The man that threw death away is not supposed to go out very far from his house, if he can help it, for four days. After the dead person has been buried, all the people, with children and all who have been in where the dead person was lying, are to go down to the river to bathe.

After that, those who wish may stay at the dead person's house for the next four days. The dead person's nearest relative, wife or husband, or if he has not either, his next nearest, sits at the place where he died.

From there he or she does not get up for four days. They remain there for four days. In the evening, before they eat their supper, they all pray together. And in the evening they do not talk about the person who has just died, but of what has happened to them in the past. So they sit around and talk as if nothing had happened. According to the belief of the people, the dead goes out of the church on the evening of the fourth day, and goes southwest toward where the sun sets, where the home of the dead is. For four days after dying it is supposed to remain in the church. And early on the fifth day, as the sun is rising, the man who threw death away comes back in with good medicine. And the people are sprinkled with this medicine by the man, he saying to them: "My people, this dead person has already gone to the home of the dead. So you must not think any more about it. You must all go to your houses with good feeling. And then you must lead a good life." As the dead person's people are told thus, they all go to their houses with good feelings.

This is a custom of the people of the Pueblo when one of their people dies.

TOKENS OF DEATH

Long ago when my grandfather was yet young, once he and two other men were going along the road near Nambé early in the morning just before it got daylight. And there was a shooting star. It passed over their heads, sparkling. Then one of the men said: "Something wrong must be thought of me as the star has passed right over our heads." Then in about one month this man died.

Once my grandfather and I were coming from the northeast along the road just before the sun set, and there was a straight strip of cloud lying to the southwest. When my grandfather saw this he said to me: "Perhaps somebody from the Pueblo is going to die; and that is the reason that the strip of cloud is lying there." And in one month a person from the Pueblo died.

Also the people say at the Pueblo that when a bird flies into a house it is bad, that something is going to happen to one of the members of the house which the bird goes into. So the people say that whenever a bird enters their house it is a bad token. Once many years ago, when I was still small, a bird flew into our house. This bird had a very big head, and also a very long beak, a small body, and a short tail. When it flew into our house we caught it and burned it up. And it was not very long after that that my grandfather died.

A MISINTERPRETED NOTE

I believe it was in the month of June, in the year 1904, but do not remember well, that at the Pueblo when the children had not yet returned from Santa Fe [Halpaane, "Shell Water"], the teacher at Picurís wanted the men to work for her in her garden, and so she wrote a note to the governor. And the note was sent to him by one of the pupils. The note was handed to the governor, and as he could neither read nor write, he took the note to a man who thought he was able to read it, to find out what the note said. The note was brought to the man by whom it was to be read. Since he did not hardly know how to read, after he got through glancing over the note he said to the governor: "This is how the teacher's note says, that you are to inform all the parents whose children are in school at Santa Fe to go down to the station at Embudo to get them, for the children who are in Santa Fe are to arrive at the station to-morrow noon." The governor, being told thus by this man, went back to his house and went up on top of the roof and shouted announcement, as it is the custom of people at the Pueblo to do when anything is going to happen or anything has been done. So he shouted announcement, telling the parents whose children are in school at Santa Fe to go down to the station of Embudo to get their children. When the people if the Pueblo heard that, the parents began to get ready.

And the next morning they went down to the station to wait. As the distance is only about 20 miles it did not take them so long to reach there. They waited at the station and the train arrived, but the school children did not come on that train. The parents returned to the Pueblo again, disappointed. And so, people, that is how an uneducated person will make trouble for us.

HUNTING THE HORSES

In the springtime at Picurís when the people are through planting some of them take their horses to the mountains so that they can get fat by eating good grass in the mountains. There they turn them loose all summer. And when fall approaches those Indians that have their horses in the mountains go there to get them so that they can work them when they are harvesting.

It was on one of these occasions that a friend of

mine and I went up to look for our horses. While we were up in the mountains we ate up all our lunch, as we did not take very much; and I sent my friend down to the Pueblo for more lunch. When he went down to get lunch I lived for three days up in the mountains just by boiling and eating some of the green herbs that grow there. Once in a while I would kill a squirrel with my gun. It was about three days after my friend brought more lunch that we found our horses. Then we took them down home again.

Rattlesnakes

At Picurís there are no rattlesnakes in the mountains. But many of them live on the plains where there are many taulone bushes. I do not know how many different kinds of rattlesnakes live there, but believe there is only one kind.

Some of the Indians at the Pueblo say that the rattlesnakes do not bite in the summer when the moon shines. But I do know this for sure: One summer evening I heard something at a distance which sounded like a cricket. Then I asked one of my friends what it was that made that noise. Then he told me that it was a rattlesnake that made that noise. I did not believe what he said, and then he told me: "If you do not believe what I say, we will go together to where the sound comes from and see." Then we went. As we reached there, with the moon shining, the snake lay coiled on a flat rock. Its rattle stuck up in the center, and when it shook the rattle it could be heard for about 2 miles away. My friend told me that this is how they call their mates. That time I discovered that the snake can use its

Mixed Animal Dance, Picuris Pueblo. Courtesy Museum of New Mexico, Neg. No. 40816.

rattle in two ways, to warn you when you get too near where it is lying, and also to call its mate.

THE BUFFALOES

The Picurís Indians used to go buffalo hunting among the plains of Mora, as the buffaloes were then plentiful there. As late as the time when my uncle was a young man, the buffaloes existed in great abundance.

I still remember him saying that he once saw them on the plains of Mora as thick as the pinyon trees that grow in the mountains. It seems strange that these animals should disappear so quickly. I suppose after guns were introduced they were all killed off.

The Indians say that the buffaloes never lived in the mountains, but they used to live on the plains, eating the grass there like cows. I believe that this is the reason that the buffaloes never lived near the Rio Grande.

Nowadays the buffalo hides are very scarce, and also the horns of the buffalo and anything else pertaining to the buffalo. These, also, are beginning to be forgotten. The hides which the Indians used in former times to put over them when they danced the buffalo dance, and those that they used in their ceremonial dances, and those that they used to spread as mats on their floors, are nowadays very rarely seen.

The following song was used by Sengerepove'ena (see note 12) and is still used by Picurís hunters for bringing deer by magical means within shooting range.

NO. 11. DEER SUMMONING SONG[42]

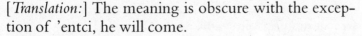

[*Translation:*] The meaning is obscure with the exception of 'entci, he will come.

Notes on the Stories

John P. Harrington
emended by Marta Weigle

Page numbers of the original (1928) Picuris language and English language texts, a list of story characters in order of their appearance, and a list of the songs precede Harrington's notes to each story. The number and title of each song is followed by the numbers and page numbers of that song's variants and by the page numbers of Helen H. Roberts's analysis of all Rosendo Vargas's renditions of that song.

Magpietail Boy and His Wife
> Original text: Picuris, 296, 298, 300, 302, 304, 306, 308, 310, 312; English, 297, 299, 301, 303, 305, 307, 309, 311, 313
> Characters: Magpietail Boy, his wife Yellow Corn Woman, Wizards, Screech Owl, Elf, Fish Maiden
> Songs: No. 1. Traveling Song of the Elf (variants 12, 13, 14, pp. 426-28; analysis, 403-4); No. 2. Love Song of the Elf (variants 15, 16, 17, pp. 429-34; analysis, 405-6)

1. It is customary to begin a Picurís myth with the words: Nakuthe nakutheke (ten) tcexamen (or with the emphatic repetition of nakuthe omitted), "long ago, long ago therefore accordingly," which may be freely rendered as "Long ago then" or "Once upon a time."

2. One of the Corn Maidens of the cardinal colors; cp. White Corn Woman, wife of Sengerepove'ena, pp. 313, 323 [i.e., "Sengerepove'ena Fights with the Sun" and "The Old Giant Steals Sengerepove'ena's Wife"].

3. One of the secret societies of Picurís.

4. For the Picurís place names the writer has in preparation a separate treatise. [Apparently, never published.]

5. *Editor's note*: Harrington's divorced wife, Carobeth Laird

(1975:82) later recalled: "Harrington also objected to the use of the word kiva to designate the underground place where Pueblo men conduct certain religious ceremonies. For some reason he preferred the Spanish estufa, employed by some of his informants. To him kiva was an artificiality for which he blamed [Bureau of American Ethnology chief] Dr. [Jesse Walter] Fewkes."

6. 'Ela-, roof-hole, N. M. Span. coye.

7. 'Elatophia-, roof-hole sticks, i.e., the sticks used for closing the roof-hole, piled beside the roof-hole when the latter is open.

8. [No translation is given for this song.]

9. The prose equivalent of the words of this song which have meaning is as follows:

	[English translation]
Hati pam'one,	Dear little flower,
Tcakwil 'a'eye	Come hither,
'Amaxutcetci.	That I may embrace thee!
Hati pam'one,	Dear little flower,
Kamantceltcisa	Let us be married,
Tepiu 'anmetci.	Come, let us go to the Pueblo.

10. "You have a tail" [Kaxweki], translated into Spanish as "Tienes cola" or "Tienes una cola." Cp. Isl. Kahwikieim, "You have a tail" or Ta kahwikieim, "Now you have a tail," etc. The narrator says this to the one whom he wants to have tell the next story.

Sengerepove'ena Fights With the Sun

Original text: Picuris, 312, 314, 316, 318, 320, 322; English, 313, 315, 317, 319, 321, 323

Characters: Sengerepove'ena, his wife, their two children (sons), Deer, people of San Juan Pueblo, Sun, the children's grandparents, Old Male Woodrat, Old Female Woodrat, White Butterflies, Black Butterflies, Yellow Butterflies, Blue Butterflies, Flying Creature (Eagle), Morning Star

11. From Tewa Sèngírípóvì'é'nú (sèngírí — as in various words of greeting, of meaning obscure to the Tewa in this name; póvì, flower; 'é'nú, youth). The stories in which Sengerepove'ena figures are felt by the Indians to be as characteristically Picurís as any of the others, yet the hero bears a Tewa name, lives at the Tewa village of San Juan, and the Tewa tell similar myths about him.

12. The butterflies of various colors are encountered by Sengerepove'ena in the order in which the cardinal directions and their colors are mentioned in Picurís ceremonies: tepupa, northeast (pathe-, white); te'opa, northwest (phon-, black); tenon, southwest (tsol-, yellow); tekwepa, southeast (tcal-, blue). To these is sometimes added: pimma, east; literally, in the middle (paxe-, gray); cp. p. 354 [now note 28].

The Old Giant Steals Sengerepove'ena's Wife
Original text: Picuris, 322, 324, 326, 328, 330; English, 323, 325, 327, 329, 331

Plate 44, "The Contest between Sengerepove'ena and the Giant," appears between pp. 327 and 328.

Characters: Sengerepove'ena, his wife White Corn Woman, Old Giant, Old Male Woodrat, Old Female Woodrat, White Butterflies, Black Butterflies, Yellow Butterflies, Blue Butterflies, Buzzard, Crow

13. For deer-summoning song used by Sengerepove'ena and other Picurís deer hunters see p. 397 [i.e., Folkways: "The Buffaloes"].

14. Proper name of the Old Giant, of obscure meaning, used by the birds, etc., in addressing him.

The Old Giantess and the Brother and Sister Fawns
Original text: Picuris, 330, 332, 334, 336, 338; English, 331, 333, 335, 337, 339

Characters: Old Giantess, Fawns (brother and sister), Old Spider Woman, Big Nostril, Old Plowmaker, Old Beaver, Snakes

15. More literally "Old Nostril" or "Nostril Old Man."

16. The more original meaning is "Digging-stick Shaper Old Man."

17. The common meaning and the one here intended by the

narrator is "plow;" the more original meaning is "digging- stick."

18. Representing the sound of hitting the plow as he shapes it.

19. A word imitative of the sound made by a drowning person.

20. Interjection of surprise.

21. Kayaipinene, Jicarita Mountain, literally "Greasy Mountain."

22. This is the way the Fawn Girl cried.

The Old Giant Steals the Elf and is Slain
Original text: Picuris, 338, 340, 342; English, 339, 341, 343
Characters: Elf, Old Giant, people's children
Songs: No. 3. Song of the Elf As He Is Packed Along (variants 18, 19, pp. 435-36; analysis, 406-8); No. 4. Song of the Elf in the Fire (variant 20, p. 437; analysis, 408-9)

23. Only the last two lines [the bottom line of music] have meaning: "A person who is very kind is carrying me on his back." [Also translated as "packing me along."]

24. Only the last two lines [the bottom line of music — d and e] have meaning: "A person who is very kind has put me in a warm place."

The Famine
Original text: Picuris, 342, 344, 346, 348; English, 343, 345, 347, 349
Characters: People of Picuris Pueblo, Picuris man and wife, their daughter and son, the daughter's two Dolls, Shell Hat, his son, Picuris man and wife who had fled to Santa Clara Pueblo

25. Archaic name probably meaning Shell Hat.

The Two Dove Maiden Sisters and the Drouth
Original text: Picuris, 348, 350; English, 349, 351
Characters: Doves (two sisters), Picuris youths, Buzzard, Crow, Morning Star Boy

The Two Dove Maiden Sisters Who Became Stars
Original text: Picuris, 350, 352; English, 351, 353
Characters: Dove Maidens (two sisters), their grandmother

Song: No. 5. Song of the Dove Maiden Sisters As They Became Stars (variant 21, p. 438; analysis, 409-10)

26. The meaning of the words is obscure except that -telhu means "she grinds."

27. Makiuto, the older sister, and Pautoke, the younger sister. Girls pray to them when they want to be strong in grinding corn.

The Woman and the Wolf
Original text: Picuris, 354; English, 355
Characters: Picuris woman, Wolf, woman's husband

28. Boxing the compass in the ceremonial order; compare p. 318, footnote [now note 12].

The Ants
Original text: Picuris, 354, 356; English, 355, 357
Characters: Ants, their leader, Eagles, Redtail Hawks, Buzzards, Turkeys, Bluebirds

29. A species of black ant.

The Sandhill Cranes
Original text: Picuris, 358, 360; English, 359, 361
Characters: Sandhill Cranes, their leader

30. Another Picurís name for Pueblo Creek.
31. Palapaane, "the Big River" (Sp. Rio Grande); also spoken of as Paane, "the River."

A Baby is Stolen by an Owl
Original text: Picuris, 360; English, 361
Characters: Pueblo woman, her baby, Owl, Pueblo man

The Sphynx Moth and the Old Coyote
Original text: Picuris, 362, 364; English, 363, 365
Characters: Sphynx Moth, his grandmother, Old Coyote, his grandmother, his children

Koyowixelapan Fetches Fire
Original text: Picuris, 364, 366, 368; English, 365, 367, 369

Characters: Koyowixelapan, her grandmother, Wizards
Songs: No. 6. Song of the Wizards as Koyowixelapan Enters
Their Estufa (variants 22, 23, pp. 439- 40; analysis, 410);
No. 7. Crying Song of the Grandmother as She Seeks
Koyowixelapan (variants 24, 25, 26, pp. 440-41; analy-
sis, 410-11); No. 8. Song of the Wizards as They Make
Koyowixelapan an Old Woman (variants 27, 28, pp.
441-42; analysis 411-12)

32. The etymology of the name is obscure.

33. [No translation for this song is given.]

34. Hayuwi is a mere filler [on p. 367: "Hajuwi has no meaning"]; the other words mean: "Koyowixelapan, I am going along
seeking you."

35. [No translation for this song is given.]

The Turkeys and the Great Flood
Original text: Picuris, 370; English, 371
Characters: Turkeys, "a certain bird," birds, three Turkey
brothers, four-footed animals, flying animals

The Origin of the Scalp House
Original text: Picuris, 370, 372; English, 371, 373
Characters: Picuris people, Taos people, Picuris man, Taos
woman and child

36. A Taos sentence in Pic. pronunciation…[Picuris text
omitted].

37. "At Night Lake," the site of the present town of Taos.

The Sunken Estufa
Original text: Picuris, 372; English 373
Characters: Picuris people

The Old Coyote Woman and the Crow Visit Each Other
Original text: Picuris, 374, 376; English, 375, 377
Characters: Crow (a woman), Old Coyote Woman, her children

38. Old Coyote Woman and Crow are old women. Cp. the
story starting p. 376 [i.e., the following story], in which Jackrab-

bit and Bluejay are old women, grinding companions of Old Coyote Woman.

39. Mutilated placename form for Tauxaitho'ai, "at Pinyon Cone Pile."

Old Coyote Woman, Jackrabbit, and Bluejay Grind Together
Original text: Picuris, 376, 378, 380; English, 377, 379, 381
Characters: Jackrabbit, Bluejay, Old Coyote Woman
Songs: No. 9. The Jackrabbit's Grinding Song (variants 29, 30, pp. 442-43; analysis, 412); No. 10. The Bluejay's Grinding Song (variants 31, 32, 33, 34, pp. 443-44; analysis, 412)

40. The words have no meaning that is understood.

41. The words have no meaning, but the syllables tsiautsiau are understood to mean "bluejay, bluejay;" cp1 tsiauene, bluejay.

The Old Coyote and the Three Gourds
Original text: Picuris, 380, 382; English, 381, 383
Characters: Gourds, Old Coyote

The Cricket and the Coyote
Original text: Picuris, 382, 384, 386; English 383, 385, 387
Characters: Cricket, Coyote, Cricket's people (Bumble Bees, White-striped Bees, Honey Bees, other winged stingers), Coyote's people (Wolves, Mountain lions, Wildcats, Bears, other beasts of prey)

Folkways: The Buffaloes
Original text: Picuris, 396; English 397

42. According to Roberts (p. 412): "The last song, No. 11 (p. 397), is not really a song, but merely a call. It was given eight times, each two being succeeded by a pause of some length. I have therefore concluded that two statements of the call naturally belonged together and formed one phrase."

Afterword

Marta Weigle

John Peabody Harrington, for thirty-nine years a linguist-ethnologist on the staff of the Smithsonian Institution's Bureau of American Ethnology (BAE), is among the most enigmatic, idiosyncratic, and prolific figures in American anthropology. Matthew W. Stirling (1963:370, 376), BAE chief from 1928 until 1957, opens his obituary by observing: "With the death of John Peabody Harrington in San Diego, California, on October 21, 1961, anthropology lost one of its most colorful personages," and concludes:

> Harrington was one of those people who became a legend during his own lifetime. The anecdotes concerning his bizarre career would fill a large volume. Most of the stories are probably true, fabulous as they sound, but all portray a very human personage — unorthodox, brilliant, humorous, generous and kind.

Harry Lawton (in Larid 1975:xxi) maintains:

> There are those who saw him as a kindly, generous man, who despite shyness possessed considerable social charm. There are just as many others who viewed him as misanthropic, opportunistic, and willing to go to any lengths to obtain more data. He seems to have made an indelible impression on everyone with whom he came in contact.

This is certainly the case with Carobeth Tucker (born in

Coleman, Texas, on July 20, 1895), who entitles the vivid, largely dismal recollections of her 1916-23 marriage (the couple had one daughter) to Harrington *Encounter with an Angry God* (Laird 1975).

Born at Waltham, Massachusetts, on April 29, 1884, to lawyer Elliott A. Harrington and his wife Mary L. Peabody, Harrington was raised in Santa Barbara, California, where his family moved when he was a young child. He studied classical languages and anthropology at Stanford University, from which he graduated at the top of his class in 1905. He did graduate work in linguistics and anthropology at the Universities of Leipzig and Berlin in 1905 and 1906 but did not complete his doctorate, later receiving an honorary Doctor of Science degree from the University of Southern California in 1934.

His first position was in California, as a teacher of modern languages at Santa Ana High School, 1907-1909. While attending summer school at the University of California at Berkeley in 1903, Harrington studied with A. L. Kroeber and Earl Pliny Goddard and began a keen, lifelong interest in California Indian languages. He undertook fieldwork on Chumash, Yuma, and Mojave languages and cultures while teaching high school. A six-week field trip to Matilda Coxe Stevenson's Black Mesa ranch in 1908 brought Harrington to the attention of BAE chief William Henry Holmes, which led to his temporary and eventually full-time work with the Bureau.

Although he taught and lectured sporadically until his appointment to the Washington, D.C., staff of the BAE on February 20, 1915 (and never thereafter), between 1909 and that date Harrington served as ethnologist under Edgar Lee Hewett at Santa Fe's School of American Archaeology (later, School of American Research) of the Archaeological Institute of America. He spent most of his time in the field studying Southwestern Indian languages, but was from September 1911 until June 1912 an assistant curator at the Museum of

John P. Harrington recording the speech of an unidentified Indian. Courtesy Museum of New Mexico, Neg. No. 88417.

New Mexico in Santa Fe. His first publication, "A Yuma Account of Origins," appeared in the 1908 volume of the *Journal of American Folklore*. Between 1908 and 1915, Harrington published fifteen articles (on Yuma, Piro, Tewa, Diegueño, Tano, Navajo, Chumash, Ute, and Paiute languages), two co-authored articles, an obituary, and two reviews in sources like the *American Anthropologist* and the Papers of the School of American Archaeology (Glemser 1963:376-77).

However, Harrington is known not for his publications but for his prodigious fieldwork on most American Indian languages, which produced massive accumulations of materials. According to Lawton (in Laird 1975:xvi):

> Harrington's monument lies in the literally tons of meticulous field notes he shipped to the Bureau of American Ethnology. It is believed that no other anthropologist ever gathered such a staggering quantity of material in the field . . . . His notes on the Chumash Indians alone filled sixty boxes. He left almost a thousand pages of notes on the Kitanemuk Serrano — about whom very little has been known up to now . . . . Even after his death in 1961, caches of manuscripts kept turning up in warehouses and depositories around the country where Harrington had stored and absent-mindedly forgotten them. The wealth of information left by Harrington is already broadening or changing our knowledge about many Indian groups, and it has been barely tapped. Ironically, Harrington's growing reputation and the increasing awareness of the greatness of his achievements rests on the use by other scholars of those notes which he always feared others were seeking to get their hands on.

Neil M. Judd (1967:46) calls Harrington "a confirmed notemaker" whose "chief weakness was his ready dismissal of what no longer interested him . . . . Across the continent, coast to coast, he had stored and forgotten uncounted reams of yellow foolscap, one note per page. Once solved, queries were left to wither." He characterizes him as

> a linguist of rare ability and rare humor. He never thought of physical comfort, either for himself or for an informant. With childlike curiosity, he would turn from a problem in hand and follow something that had attracted his attention until he ran it to earth. Then he might return to the abandoned problem or he might forget it. Such was his uncanny ability even with a new language that he could, within a week, correct an informant's errors in his own tongue. During war years Harrington was frequently called upon to translate letters and messages in unfamiliar script for the State, War, and Navy departments.

Harrington retired from the BAE on April 30, 1954, and was then appointed a research associate of the Smithsonian Institution to continue his linguistic studies.

Because he was very secretive about his work and whereabouts, and cryptic or laconic about context and informant in his notes and publications, it is difficult to document Harrington's career, as it relates to Picuris Pueblo or any other group. Fiscal-year, *Annual Reports of the Board of Regents of The Smithsonian Institution* contain useful material in the appended Reports of the BAE. According to BAE chief Jesse Walter Fewkes's report for the fiscal year ending June 30, 1921 (*Smithsonian Annual Report*, p. 63): "Upon finishing the manuscript of the Kiowa paper [Harrington 1928], Mr. Harrington took up the Taos material, aided by a set of excellent texts dictated by Mr. R. Vargas, and comprising 400 typewritten pages. He finished this for publication before the close of the fiscal year."

In his first paper on the Tiwa language, Harrington (1910:15) had noted: "When Taos and Picuris people talk together, Tiwa is used, these two dialects differing as little from one another as do the dialects of the Tewa pueblos." That paper was based on fieldwork with three Taos Pueblo informants: Manuel Mondragon, José Lopez, and Santiago Mirabal. "Most of the material was obtained from the informant first mentioned. His Indian name is T'öltö, Sun Elk. He is a patient fellow and is deeply interested in the recording of his language" (Harrington 1910:17). Carobeth Laird (1975:69) recalls the two of them working with Mondragon at Taos Pueblo in 1918:

> The informant whom Harrington finally secured (I believe he had worked with him before) was named Manuel. He was a dour, silent man with black braids framing his dark face and falling down over the immaculate white sheet in which he draped himself. His moccasins were always impeccably whitened. He had little rapport with Harrington, even less with me. He answered questions with great deliberation, and, I am sure, accurately, but he volunteered very little.

Presumably, Rosendo Vargas of Picuris Pueblo was interviewed by Harrington in 1918, but whether at Picuris or Taos is unknown. Besides what he writes about Vargas in his introduction to "Picurís Children's Stories," Harrington (p. 293) notes the latter's "Indian name Phithexomene (shortened familiarly to Thexon), Feather-bunch Flying (phi- from phi'ine, feather-bunch, Spanish plumero; thexomene, that which flies or floats along in the air, from thexome-, to fly along, -ne, agentive)."

Fewkes mentions in his report for the fiscal year ending on June 30, 1923, that "the 12 [11 in this part of the paper] songs accompanying the stories are beautifully rendered by Mr. Rosendo Vargas, and are transcribed into musical notation by Miss H. H. Roberts" (*Smithsonian Annual Report*, p. 69). Helen Heffron Roberts was born in Chicago, Illinois, in 1888. A graduate of Chicago Musical College, she did post-graduate work at the American Conservatory in 1914 and received an M.A. in anthropology from Columbia University in 1919. The Picuris work seems to have been done between Roberts's 1920-21 field trip to collect Jamaican folksongs sponsored by the Folklore Foundation of Vassar College and the American Association for the Advancement of Science, a 1922 field trip to central California, and a 1923-24 field survey for the Hawaiian Legend and Folklore Commission. In 1924, she became a research assistant in anthropology at Yale University, where she remained at least until 1938, when she claimed to be "interested in anthropology and primitive and exotic music; [with] research underway on Nootka Indian music, on music of the Southwest U.S., on California Indian music, on natural history of the Conch trumpet" (National Research Council 1938:83).

When Fewkes announced that Harrington had read proofs of the Picuris article during the fiscal year ending June 30, 1927 (*Smithsonian Annual Report*, p. 69), he reported: "In connection with the Picuris paper, Miss H. H. Roberts prepared transcriptions and analyses of Picuris songs which will constitute the most complete study in existence of the music of this tribe." In her "Analysis of Picurís Songs" (pp. 399-447), Roberts claims that their importance is basically "that they are, I believe, the first collection of Indian, or, for that matter, of any exotic songs ever so studied where all were sung by one individual and where several additional renditions (from one to four) were secured of each." Furthermore, ". . . another good point is that the songs are all of one type, that is, they all belong with myths. Therefore if any stylistic feature is common to myth songs as a group, it should be discoverable" (p. 399). She concludes her analysis of the eleven songs and their twenty- three variants with a discussion of the "Scales of the Songs" (pp. 414-25) and musical transcriptions of those scales (pp. 445-47).

Helen H. Roberts earlier published the Picuris words and versions of her musical transcriptions to two songs in "Picurís Children's Stories": No. 2 ("Love Song of the Elf,

Magpie-Tail-Boy Myth") and No. 4 ("Song of the Elf in the Fire, Old Giant Myth") — both noted as collected by J. P. Harrington and "reproduced by permission of the BAE" — in her 1927 *Natural History* article, "Indian Music from the Southwest." She notes that "a number of myth songs taken by him in the village of Picurís and transcribed by the writer, are now in press" (Roberts 1927:262). Roberts herself made field trips to study Pueblo music in 1929 and 1930, but she appears to have been working in Washington and/or Chicago and New York in 1922-23, judging from her articles published at this time.

Despite their 1928 appearance as daunting, bilingual texts with a single story illustration (Plate 44), "Picurís Children's Stories" evidently were intended for children as well as scholars, according to Fewkes's report for the fiscal year ending June 10, 1923 (*Smithsonian Annual Report*, pp. 68-69):

> This manuscript embraces Picurís stories in native text such as are told to the Indian children on winter evenings in their little isolated village in northern New Mexico. The stories have high literary quality, and many of them hold the attention of child or adult throughout. The volume is thought to be practical for school use.

However, it is not listed as a children's book in the bibliography of North American Indian folklore prepared by the Children's Book Section of the Library of Congress and appears only as a source: "Although presented as children's stories, there is nothing to suggest that the tales belong especially to children" (Ullom 1969:104). (It might be noted here that Harrington, with Robert W. Young, later did the Navajo linguisitics for four bilingual children's books by Ann Nolan Clark, published by the U.S. Office of Indian Affairs: *Little Herder in Autumn* [1940; reprinted by Ancient City Press in 1988], *Who Wants To Be a Prairie Dog?* [1940], *Little Herder in Summer* [1942], and *Little Herder in Winter* [1942].)

In his obituary for John Peabody Harrington Matthew

W. Stirling (1963:375) marvels at the linguist's "phenomenal memory of detail" and proposes: "Certainly no linguist was ever acquainted with so many American Indian languages over so wide a territory." He states that Harrington showed little interest in theory or grammatical analysis but much concern for vocabularies, texts, and place name etymologies. Stirling (1963:371) notes: "In later years I have heard both A. L. Kroeber and Edward Sapir state that Harrington probably had the best ear for phonetics of any American linguist." Although "always much interested in new mechanical and electronic developments for recording sound, both auditory and graphic,"

> Harrington never gave up his own phonetic orthography and did not adopt the phonemic approach. Like other long-time B.A.E. staff members, his immersion in his own research put him outside the stream of development of linguistic and ethnological methods and interests. The value of his materials — other than the absolute value of any materials on now-extinct languages — lies principally in their phonetic accuracy (which has been demonstrated by modern work on some of the same language, such as Karok) . . . . He felt that his most important task was rescuing from oblivion information that otherwise would be forever lost. For this reason, he was little interested in publication and begrudged the time required to put manuscripts in shape for this purpose. His satisfaction came from putting the data on record. (Stirling 1963:373-74)

Harrington was not concerned with the stories and folkways accounts as folklore, in this case narratives and songs of particular genres with cross-cultural relationships. Thus, he did not organize the tales into categories like origin tales, hero tales, novelistic tales, animal tales, European stories, and true stories, as Ruth Benedict does in her *Tales of the Cochiti Indians* (1931). Nor does he provide summaries, analysis, and comparative discussion like Benedict or several variants of each tale and numerous explanatory and comparative footnotes as Elsie Clews Parsons does in her *Taos Tales* (1940). Instead, he deplores the omission of interlinear translation, which "best serves the purpose for which such texts are published" (p. 294), due to printing costs, settling for facing Picuris and English texts. Nevertheless, published in English versions only and enhanced by Helen H. Roberts's musical transcriptions, John P. Harrington's "Picurís Children's Stories, with Texts and Songs," collected from Rosendo Vargas, are welcome and intriguing additions to our knowledge of traditional American Indian literature and lore.

References

Benedict, Ruth
  1931 Tales of the Cochiti Indians. Bulletin of the Bureau of American Ethnology 98. Washington: Government Printing Office.
Brown, Donald N.
  1979 Picuris Pueblo. *In* Handbook of North American Indians, Vol. 9: Southwest, ed. Alfonso Ortiz, pp. 268–77. Washington, D.C.: Smithsonian Institution.
  1980 Dance as Experience: the Deer Dance of Picuris Pueblo. *In* Southwestern Indian Ritual Drama, ed. Charlotte J. Frisbie, pp. 71-92. School of American Research Advanced Seminar Series. Albuquerque: University of New Mexico Press.
Glemser, Karlena, comp.
  1963 Bibliography of the Writings of John Peabody Harrington. American Anthropologist 65:376-81.

Harrington, John P.

1910 An Introductory Paper on the Tiwa Language, Dialect of Taos, New Mexico. American Anthropologist 12:11-48.

1928 Vocabulary of the Kiowa Language. Bulletin of the Bureau of American Ethnology 84. Washington: Government Printing Office.

Harrington, John P., and Helen H. Roberts

1928 Picurís Children's Stories, with Texts and Songs. Forty-third Annual Report of the Bureau of American Ethnology to the Secretary of the Smithsonian Institution, 1925-1926, by J. Walter Fewkes, Chief, pp. 289-447. Washington: Government Printing Office.

Judd, Neil M.

1967 The Bureau of American Ethnology: A Partial History. Norman: University of Oklahoma Press.

Laird, Carobeth

1975 Encounter with an Angry God: Recollections of My Life with John Peabody Harrington. Morongo Indian Reservation, Banning, California: Malki Museum Press.

National Research Council

1938 International Directory of Anthropologists. Washington, D.C.

Parsons, Elsie Clews

1940 Taos Tales. Memoirs of the American Folk-Lore Society, Vol. 34. New York: J. J. Augustin for the American Folk-Lore Society.

Roberts, Helen H.

1927 Indian Music from the Southwest. Natural History 27:257-65.

Schroeder, Albert H.

1974 A Brief History of Picuris Pueblo: A Tiwa Indian Group in North Central New Mexico. Adams State College Series in Anthropology, No. 2. (February 1). Alamosa, Colorado.

Stirling, M. W.
    1963 John Peabody Harrington, 1884–1961 [obituary].
         American Anthropologist 65:370-76.

Ullom, Judith C., comp.
    1969 Folklore of the North American Indians: An An-
         notated Bibliography. Washington, D.C.: Library
         of Congress.